Concentrations of Polycyclic Aromatic Hydrocarbons (PAHs) in Urban Stormwater, Madison, Wisconsin, 2005–08

By William R. Selbig

In cooperation with the Wisconsin Department of Natural Resources and the Minnesota Pollution Control Agency

Open-File Report 2009–1077

U.S. Department of the Interior
U.S. Geological Survey

U.S. Department of the Interior
KEN SALAZAR, Secretary

U.S. Geological Survey
Suzette M. Kimball, Acting Director

U.S. Geological Survey, Reston, Virginia: 2009

For more information on the USGS—the Federal source for science about the Earth, its natural and living resources, natural hazards, and the environment, visit http://www.usgs.gov or call 1-888-ASK-USGS

For an overview of USGS information products, including maps, imagery, and publications, visit http://www.usgs.gov/pubprod

To order this and other USGS information products, visit http://store.usgs.gov

Suggested citation:
Selbig, W.R., 2009, Concentrations of polycyclic aromatic hydrocarbons (PAHs) in urban stormwater, Madison, Wisconsin, 2005–08: U.S. Geological Survey Open-File Report 2009–1077, 46 p.

Contents

Figures

Tables

Conversion Factors and Abbreviations

Multiply	By	To obtain
Length		
inch (in.)	2.54	centimeter (cm)
foot (ft)	0.3048	meter (m)
Area		
acre	0.4047	hectare (ha)
square foot (ft^2)	0.09290	square meter (m^2)
Volume		
liter (L)	0.2642	gallon (gal)

Temperature in degrees Celsius (°C) may be converted to degrees Fahrenheit (°F) as follows °F=(1.8×°C)+32

Horizontal coordinate information is referenced to the 1991 adjustment of the North American Datum of 1983 (NAD 83/91).

Water year in USGS reports is the 12-month period October 1 through September 30. The water year is designated by the calendar year in which it ends.

Concentrations of Polycyclic Aromatic Hydrocarbons (PAHs) in Urban Stormwater, Madison, Wisconsin, 2005–08

By William R. Selbig

Abstract

Concentrations of 18 PAH compounds were characterized from six urban source areas (parking lots, feeder street, collector street, arterial street, rooftop, and strip mall) around Madison, Wisconsin. Parking lots were categorized into those that were or were not sealed. On average, chrysene, fluoranthene, and pyrene were the dominant PAH compounds in all urban stormwater samples. Geometric mean concentrations for most individual PAH compounds were significantly greater for a parking lot that was sealed than for lots that were not sealed. Results from this study are consistent with similar studies that measured PAH concentrations in urban stormwater samples in Marquette, Mich., and Madison, Wis.

Introduction

Environmental managers are often faced with the difficult challenge of developing strategies to mitigate a variety of pollutants entrained in urban runoff. Characterizing pollutant concentrations by source area may help focus managerial decision-making. Limited attention has been given to more unconventional and potentially toxic pollutants, such as polycyclic aromatic hydrocarbons (PAHs), owing to a lack of concentration data. Although there is growing evidence that PAHs and other organic pollutants are degrading the health of urban water resources, not enough data are available to do a mass balance on their sources.

In 2005, the U.S. Geological Survey (USGS), in cooperation with the Wisconsin Department of Natural Resources (WDNR), began a study to help municipalities reduce the uncertainty in their stormwater management planning by characterizing polycyclic aromatic hydrocarbon (PAH) concentrations in urban runoff from different source areas and land uses. As part of an interstate cooperative agreement, the Minnesota Pollution Control Agency (MPCA) joined the study in 2008. Water-quality samples were collected at multiple sites in Madison, Wis., for approximately 1 year at each site; the entire study spanned August 2005 through September 2008. The purpose of this report is to summarize PAH concentration data collected from six urban source areas in or near Madison, Wis., during the study and to compare these data to PAH concentrations reported in previous studies.

Description of Study Areas

This study characterized concentrations of individual PAH compounds as well as a total PAH summation from several urban source areas. Specific source areas and land-use categories are identified in table 1. Choice of these urban source areas was based on the prevalence of the specific types of source areas within urban watersheds. Data from source areas or land uses with multiple sampling locations were synthesized to represent their respective category. For example, data from three different commercial parking lots were synthesized into a single dataset representing all parking lots. Parking lots were further delineated by maintenance criteria as being either sealed or not sealed with an asphalt or coal-tar-based sealant. Each street was categorized by traffic volume as a feeder, collector, or arterial street. A summary of the geographic setting and physical description for each study area follows.

Table 1. Source areas and land uses sampled for definition of pollutant concentration.

Source area	Land use	Number of sites
Parking lot	Commercial	3 (1 sealed, 2 not sealed)
Streets	Residential, commercial	3
Rooftop	Institutional (flat)	1
Mixed use	Commercial (strip mall)	1

Parking Lot 1

Figures 1A and 1B illustrate the layout and general appearance of parking lot 1. This 3.3-acre commercial parking area is on the west side of Madison adjacent to a home improvement store. The asphalt-based surface was approximately 10 to 15 years old at the time of study. Maintenance of the asphalt lot has been limited to periodic sealing of cracks with an asphalt-based tar. Runoff is collected into a single storm-sewer inlet near the center of the parking lot, then conveyed through a concrete, 30-in.-diameter circular pipe from which the runoff eventually drains into an open ditch.

Figure 1.   Parking lot number 1.
A, Ground-level view.
B, Aerial view with delineated drainage boundary.

Parking Lot 2

Figures 2A and 2B illustrate the layout and general appearance of parking lot 2. This 5.9-acre commercial parking area is on the east side of Madison adjacent to a shopping center complex. The asphalt-based surface was approximately 5 years old at the time of study. Maintenance of the asphalt lot has been limited to periodic sealing of cracks with an asphalt-based tar. Runoff is collected into multiple storm-sewer inlets then conveyed through a common concrete, 36-in.-diameter circular pipe, from which the runoff eventually drains into a detention pond.

EXPLANATION

☐ Drainage basin

0 50 100 200 Feet

0 25 50 Meters

Figure 2. Parking lot number 2.
A, Ground-level view.
B, Aerial view with delineated drainage boundary.

Parking Lot 3

A

B

Figures 3*A* and 3*B* illustrate the layout and general appearance of parking lot 3. This 0.91-acre parking lot is used primarily for employees of an electric generation plant during weekdays and as overflow parking for nearby businesses during weeknights and weekends (Judy Horwatich, U.S. Geological Survey, written commun., 2009). The asphalt-based surface was 22 years old at the time of study. Maintenance for the parking lot includes periodic application of seal coat. A seal coat of coal-tar was last applied in 2000.

Figure 3.   Parking lot number 3. *A*, Ground-level view. *B*, Aerial view with delineated drainage boundary.

Feeder Street

This 0.4-acre residential street had an average daily traffic count of fewer than 1,500 vehicles per day at the time of study. Runoff from the asphalt-based street is collected via concrete curb and gutter and conveyed into a nearby storm sewer. Runoff is from the street surface with no additional contributing source areas. A moderate amount of organic detritus is deposited on the street surface from overhead tree canopy, especially during spring and fall. The street was cleaned monthly during the study period, commencing in early spring and ending in late fall. Figure 4 shows the general appearance of the residential feeder street.

Figure 4.   Feeder street, Madison, Wis.

Collector Street

This 0.93-acre commercial street had an average daily traffic count ranging between 10,000 to 15,000 vehicles per day at the time of study, designating it as a collector to minor arterial street. Runoff from the asphalt-based street is collected from two lanes of asphalt pavement in both the eastbound and westbound directions via concrete curb and gutter and then conveyed into a concrete, 15-in.-diameter circular pipe. Streets are the major source of runoff; even though a grassed median separates the eastbound and westbound lanes, it was not considered a significant source of runoff. The street was cleaned monthly during the study period, commencing in early spring and ending in late fall. Figure 5 shows the general appearance of the collector street.

Figure 5. Collector (minor arterial) street, Middleton, Wis.

Arterial Street

A

B

EXPLANATION

☐ Eastbound lanes drainage basin
☐ Westbound lanes drainage basin

The arterial street is a length of U.S. Highway 151 in Madison, Wis. It was reconstructed in 1999 as divided highway with up to four lanes in each direction. The monitored stretch of highway has a drainage area of 2.27 acres and approximately 5,000 linear feet of curb and gutter that directs highway runoff into a concrete, 18-in.-diameter circular pipe (Judy Horwatich, U.S. Geological Survey, written commun., 2009). A 3-ft-wide grassed median separates the eastbound and westbound lanes. Runoff from a small, grassy hillside drains to the arterial street but was not considered a significant source of flow (Judy Horwatich, U.S. Geological Survey, oral commun., 2009). The concrete-based highway has 1/8-in. grooves oriented perpendicular to traffic flow. These grooves provide pavement drainage and traction for vehicles under slippery conditions. Average daily traffic count was approximately 40,000 vehicles per day at the time of study. Figures 6*A* and 6*B* show the general appearance of the arterial street.

Figure 6. Arterial street. *A*, Ground-level view. *B*, Aerial view with delineated drainage boundary.

Commercial Roof

The commercial roof monitored as part of this study is a municipal wellhouse on the west side of Madison, Wis. Runoff from the 3,080-ft² flat, rubber roof is directed equally to one of two aluminum downspouts. Samples were acquired at the end of a single downspout. Figure 7 shows the general appearance of the commercial roof.

Figure 7.   Commercial roof, Madison, Wis.

Mixed-Use Area (Strip Mall)

This 2.76-acre mixed-use area (representing the "strip mall" category sometimes used in urban stormwater studies and models) is in the City of Fitchburg, just south of Madison. Runoff originates from four primary source areas: parking lot (57 percent), roofs (24 percent), sidewalks (15 percent), and grassed areas (4 percent). Runoff is collected by multiple storm-sewer inlets and then conveyed through a single concrete, 12-in.-diameter circular storm sewer, from which the runoff eventually drains into an open ditch. Roofs within the strip-mall drainage basin are constructed primarily with asphalt composite shingles commonly found on residential dwellings. The gutters and downspouts are constructed primarily of painted extruded aluminum. The asphalt-based parking lot was approximately 10 years old at the time of study, having been constructed in 1999. Maintenance for the parking lot has included periodic application of seal coat. Sealant was last applied on July 16, 2008, at approximately halfway through the sampling timeframe of this study. It is unknown whether the sealant was asphalt or coal-tar based. Figures 8A and 8B show the general appearance and layout of the strip mall.

A

B

Drainage basin

Figure 8. Mixed use (strip mall) study site, Fitchburg, Wis. *A*, Ground-level view. *B*, Aerial view with delineated drainage boundary.

Runoff-Sample Collection

An automated monitoring station was used to measure flow and collect samples near the basin outlet of each source area monitored in this study. Each monitoring station was equipped with automated stormwater-quality samplers and instruments to measure water level and velocity. Measurement, control, and storage of data were done by way of electronic dataloggers. Precipitation data were collected by use of a tipping-bucket rain gage calibrated to 0.01 inch. A probe with two different sensor systems was mounted to the bottom of each pipe. Each probe contained a pressure transducer to measure water level and a pair of ultrasonic transducers to measure velocity. A fifth-order polynomial was used to convert water level into cross-sectional area for each pipe configuration. Instantaneous pipe discharge was then computed by multiplying the cross-sectional area of the pipe by the associated mean velocity. Storm-runoff volumes were computed by summing the 1-minute-interval instantaneous discharge during the sampled storm.

Sample collection was activated by a rise in water level in the pipe during a precipitation event. Once the water-level threshold was exceeded, typically a depth of 0.15 ft from the pipe floor, the volume of water passing the station was measured and accumulated at 1-minute increments until a volumetric threshold was reached. At that point, the sampler collected a discrete water sample and the volumetric counter was reset. The process was repeated until the water level receded below the threshold. The Teflon-lined intake nozzle of the sampler orifice was approximately 0.5 in. above the pipe floor. Subsamples, 1 L in volume, were transferred through the Teflon-lined sample tubing into a 10-L glass jar.

These flow-weighted samples were collected and composited into a single water sample, then split and processed for analysis. A Teflon churn splitter was used to composite and split samples into smaller, 1-L amber glass bottles for detection of PAH compounds. Processed samples were kept in a refrigerator at 4°C until delivered to the analytical laboratory, usually within 48 hours after runoff cessation. Because each discrete sample was composited into a single event sample, the resulting concentrations represent the event mean concentration (EMC). Samples were analyzed at the Wisconsin State Laboratory of Hygiene, in Madison.

Results

Table 2 lists individual PAH compounds for which samples were analyzed and the detection frequency for each source area or land use. The parking-lot source area was divided into lots that were or were not sealed with an asphalt or coal-tar-based sealant. A detection frequency of "none," "intermittent," or "common" indicates that concentrations in all, more than 50 percent, or fewer than 50 percent of the samples analyzed were below the detection limit for the corresponding PAH compound, respectively.

Of the 18 individual PAH compounds for which samples were analyzed, 6 were nearly always below the detection limit for all source areas monitored: acenaphthylene, dibenzo (A, H) anthracene, fluorene, 1-methylnaphthalene, 2-methylnaphthalene, and naphthalene. In most cases, individual PAH compounds that were never detected in runoff from the roof, the streets, or the mixed-use area were intermittently detected in runoff from parking lots. On average, chrysene, fluoranthene, and pyrene were the dominant PAH compounds in all urban stormwater samples (fig. 9). This finding is consistent with results from similar, previous studies that measured PAH concentrations in urban stormwater samples (Hoffman, 1985; Steuer and others, 1996,1997; Menzie and others, 2002; Stein and others, 2006).

Table 2.   Limits of detection and detection frequencies of polycyclic aromatic hydrocarbons.

[μg/L, micrograms per liter]

Polycyclic aromatic hydrocarbon	Limit of detection (μg/L)	Detection frequency						
		Parking lots		Roof	Streets			Mixed
		Sealant	No sealant		Feeder	Collector	Arterial	Strip mall
Acenaphthene	0.06	Intermittent	Intermittent	None	None	Intermittent	Intermittent	None
Acenaphthylene	.11	None	None	None	None	None	None	None
Anthracene	.03	Common	Intermittent	Intermittent	Intermittent	Intermittent	Common	None
Benzo (A) Anthracene	.093	Common	Common	Common	Intermittent	Common	Common	Common
Benzo (A) Pyrene	.160	Common	Common	Common	Intermittent	Common	Common	Common
Benzo (B) Fluoranthene	.130	Common	Common	Common	Intermittent	Common	Common	Common
Benzo (G,H,I,) Perylene	.140	Common	Common	Common	Intermittent	Common	Common	Common
Benzo (K) Fluoranthene	.120	Common	Common	Intermittent	Intermittent	Common	Common	Common
Chrysene	.027	Common	Common	Common	Common	Common	Common	Common
Dibenzo (A, H) Anthracene	.03	Intermittent	Intermittent	None	None	None	None	None
Fluoranthene	.110	Common	Common	Common	Intermittent	Common	Common	Common
Fluorene	.52	None	Intermittent	None	None	None	None	None
Indeno (1.2.3-C,D) Pyrene	.093	Common	Common	Common	Intermittent	Common	Common	Common
1-Methylnaphthalene	.06	None	None	None	None	None	None	None
2-Methylnaphthalene	.05	Intermittent	None	None	None	Intermittent	None	None
Naphthalene	.04	None	None	None	None	Intermittent	Intermittent	None
Phenanthrene	.093	Common	Common	Common	Intermittent	Common	Common	Common
Pyrene	.110	Common	Common	Common	Intermittent	Common	Common	Common

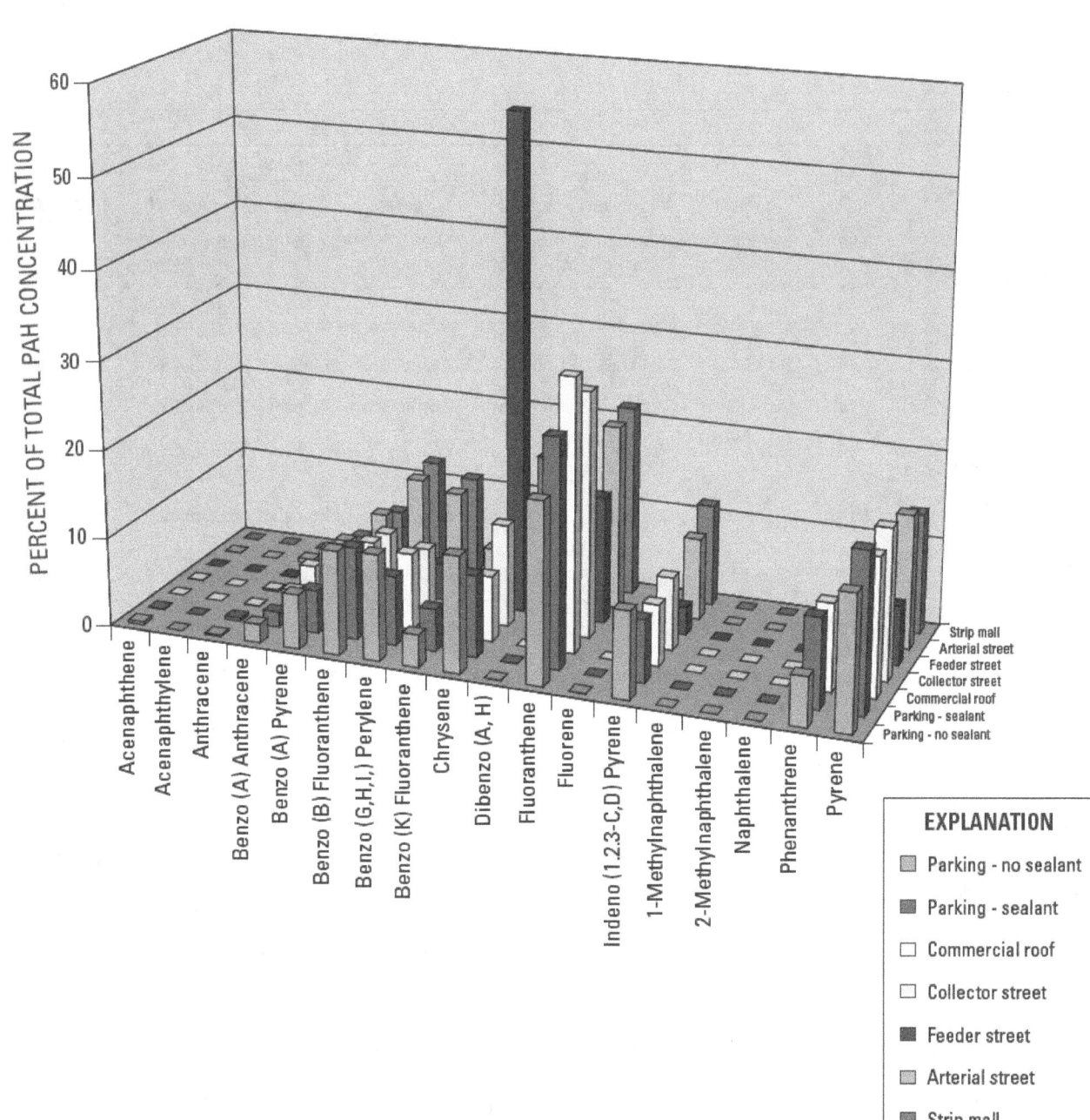

Figure 9.   Percent contribution of individual PAH compounds from source areas monitored in Madison, Wis. (2008).

Table 3A. Summary statistics of polycyclic aromatic hydrocarbons for parking lots that have and have not been sealed.

[<, less than; —, not determined; µg/L, micrograms per liter; chemical nomenclature is that of the Wisconsin State Laboratory of Hygiene]

Polycyclic aromatic hydrocarbon	Number of observations	Number of detections	Minimum (µg/L)	Maximum (µg/L)	Median (µg/L)	Mean (µg/L)	Standard deviation	Coefficient of variation
Parking lot—Sealed								
Acenaphthene	14	6	<.064	0.17	<.064	0.09	0.04	0.41
Acenaphthylene	15	0	<0.11	<0.11	<0.11	—	—	—
Anthracene	13	12	0.05	0.35	0.25	0.22	0.10	0.45
Benzo (A) Anthracene	14	11	0.17	2.00	1.10	1.09	0.71	0.65
Benzo (A) Pyrene	13	13	0.66	6.10	3.60	3.21	1.86	0.58
Benzo (B) Fluoranthene	15	15	1.70	10.00	5.20	5.55	2.49	0.45
Benzo (G,H,I,) Perylene	15	15	1.20	7.40	4.10	4.19	1.87	0.44
Benzo (K) Fluoranthene	15	15	0.68	4.80	2.40	2.56	1.19	0.47
Chrysene	15	15	1.40	8.80	4.70	4.93	2.17	0.44
Dibenzo (A, H) Anthracene	15	1	<0.12	0.47	<0.12	—	—	—
Fluoranthene	15	15	3.70	25.00	13.00	13.81	6.17	0.45
Fluorene	15	0	<0.52	<0.52	<0.52	—	—	—
Indeno (1.2.3-C,D) Pyrene	15	15	1.10	6.20	3.80	3.75	1.60	0.43
1-Methylnaphthalene	15	0	<0.064	<0.064	<0.064	—	—	—
2-Methylnaphthalene	15	4	<0.049	0.11	<0.049	0.06	0.02	0.34
Naphthalene	15	0	<0.042	<0.042	<0.042	—	—	—
Phenanthrene	15	15	1.40	11.00	5.20	5.41	2.56	0.47
Pyrene	15	15	2.50	17.00	9.20	9.65	4.33	0.45
Total PAH	15	15	14.56	95.56	52.33	53.86	23.98	0.45

Table 3A continues on the next page.

Tables 3A through 3F detail summary statistics for individual and total PAH concentrations. Descriptive statistics for datasets with censored values (values reported as less than the laboratory's limit of detection) were calculated by use of the nonparametric Kaplan-Meier method (Helsel, 2005). Total PAHs are the sum of individual, uncensored PAH compounds for each analyzed sample. Concentrations of PAH compounds for each sampled precipitation event are detailed in appendix tables 1–1 through 1–7.

Table 3A. Summary statistics of polycyclic aromatic hydrocarbons for parking lots that have and have not been sealed—Continued.

[<, less than; —, not determined; µg/L, micrograms per liter; chemical nomenclature is that of the Wisconsin State Laboratory of Hygiene]

Polycyclic aromatic hydrocarbon	Number of observations	Number of detections	Minimum (µg/L)	Maximum (µg/L)	Median (µg/L)	Mean (µg/L)	Standard deviation	Coefficient of variation
Parking lots—Not sealed								
Acenaphthene	27	2	<0.064	0.30	<0.064	—	—	—
Acenaphthylene	27	0	<0.11	<0.11	<0.11	—	—	—
Anthracene	27	6	<0.031	1.30	<0.031	0.09	0.25	2.63
Benzo (A) Anthracene	27	16	<0.093	3.60	0.17	0.36	0.69	1.91
Benzo (A) Pyrene	27	22	<0.16	5.00	0.35	0.62	0.97	1.55
Benzo (B) Fluoranthene	27	25	<0.13	6.10	0.54	0.93	1.22	1.31
Benzo (G,H,I,) Perylene	27	26	<0.14	5.00	0.53	0.84	1.00	1.20
Benzo (K) Fluoranthene	27	19	<0.12	2.90	0.24	0.43	0.57	1.32
Chrysene	27	27	0.04	5.70	0.43	0.77	1.13	1.47
Dibenzo (A, H) Anthracene	27	1	<0.034	0.10	<0.034	—	—	—
Fluoranthene	27	26	<0.11	16.00	1.05	1.94	3.17	1.64
Fluorene	27	1	<0.52	0.65	<0.52	—	—	—
Indeno (1.2.3-C,D) Pyrene	27	26	<0.093	4.00	0.43	0.70	0.83	1.18
1-Methylnaphthalene	27	0	<0.064	<0.064	<0.064	—	—	—
2-Methylnaphthalene	27	0	<0.049	<0.049	<0.049	—	—	—
Naphthalene	27	0	<0.042	<0.042	<0.042	—	—	—
Phenanthrene	27	20	<0.093	8.70	0.31	0.80	1.68	2.10
Pyrene	27	26	<0.11	12.00	0.77	1.43	2.37	1.66
Total PAH	27	27	4.98	71.25	4.76	8.62	13.96	1.62

Table 3*B.* Summary statistics of polycyclic aromatic hydrocarbons for residential feeder street.

[<, less than; —, not determined; μg/L, micrograms per liter; chemical nomenclature is that of the Wisconsin State Laboratory of Hygiene]

Polycyclic aromatic hydrocarbon	Number of observations	Number of detections	Minimum (μg/L)	Maximum (μg/L)	Median (μg/L)	Mean (μg/L)	Standard deviation	Coefficient of variation
Acenaphthene	15	0	<0.064	<0.064	<0.064	—	—	—
Acenaphthylene	15	0	<0.11	<0.11	<0.11	—	—	—
Anthracene	15	1	<0.031	0.05	<0.031	—	—	—
Benzo (A) Anthracene	15	5	<0.093	0.58	<0.093	0.18	0.15	0.85
Benzo (A) Pyrene	15	5	<0.16	0.85	<0.16	0.29	0.23	0.78
Benzo (B) Fluoranthene	15	5	<0.13	1.30	<0.13	0.33	0.36	1.08
Benzo (G,H,I,) Perylene	14	5	<0.14	1.10	<0.14	0.33	0.32	0.96
Benzo (K) Fluoranthene	15	4	<0.12	0.40	<0.12	0.17	0.09	0.54
Chrysene	15	12	<0.027	1.00	0.06	0.23	0.32	1.38
Dibenzo (A, H) Anthracene	15	0	<0.034	<0.034	<0.034	—	—	—
Fluoranthene	13	6	<0.11	2.70	<0.11	0.64	0.83	1.31
Fluorene	15	0	<0.52	<0.52	<0.52	—	—	—
Indeno (1.2.3-C,D) Pyrene	15	4	<0.093	0.86	<0.093	0.21	0.24	1.11
1-Methylnaphthalene	15	0	<0.064	<0.064	<0.064	—	—	—
2-Methylnaphthalene	15	0	<0.049	<0.049	<0.049	—	—	—
Naphthalene	15	0	<0.042	<0.042	<0.042	—	—	—
Phenanthrene	15	5	<0.093	1.30	<0.093	0.31	0.38	1.26
Pyrene	13	5	<0.11	1.90	<0.11	0.50	0.61	1.22
Total PAH	15	15	0	11.13	0.05	2.16	3.86	1.79

Table 3C.   Summary statistics of polycyclic aromatic hydrocarbons for collector street.

[<, less than; —, not determined; µg/L, micrograms per liter; chemical nomenclature is that of the Wisconsin State Laboratory of Hygiene]

Polycyclic aromatic hydrocarbon	Number of observations	Number of detections	Minimum (µg/L)	Maximum (µg/L)	Median (µg/L)	Mean (µg/L)	Standard deviation	Coefficient of variation
Acenaphthene	17	2	<0.064	0.22	<0.064	—	—	—
Acenaphthylene	17	0	<0.11	<0.11	<0.11	—	—	—
Anthracene	17	3	<0.031	0.42	<0.031	—	—	—
Benzo (A) Anthracene	17	11	<0.093	2.20	0.14	0.39	0.59	1.52
Benzo (A) Pyrene	17	11	<0.16	2.90	0.29	0.62	0.90	1.46
Benzo (B) Fluoranthene	17	12	<0.13	4.50	0.42	0.80	1.23	1.54
Benzo (G,H,I,) Perylene	17	12	<0.14	3.60	0.36	0.66	0.95	1.44
Benzo (K) Fluoranthene	17	9	<0.12	2.10	0.20	0.37	0.53	1.45
Chrysene	17	16	<0.027	3.70	0.39	0.66	1.03	1.56
Dibenzo (A, H) Anthracene	17	0	<0.034	<0.034	<0.034	—	—	—
Fluoranthene	17	16	<0.11	9.60	0.93	1.72	2.80	1.63
Fluorene	17	0	<0.52	<0.52	<0.52	—	—	—
Indeno (1.2.3-C,D) Pyrene	17	13	<0.093	2.90	0.31	0.59	0.87	1.47
1-Methylnaphthalene	17	0	<0.064	<0.064	<0.064	—	—	—
2-Methylnaphthalene	17	2	<0.049	0.12	<0.049	—	—	—
Naphthalene	17	1	<0.042	0.06	<0.042	—	—	—
Phenanthrene	17	12	<0.093	4.50	0.33	0.78	1.37	1.75
Pyrene	17	15	<0.11	7.10	0.69	1.25	2.03	1.62
Total PAH	15	15	0	42.92	1.83	5.74	12.47	2.17

Table 3D. Summary statistics of polycyclic aromatic hydrocarbons for arterial street.

[<, less than; —, not determined; µg/L, micrograms per liter; chemical nomenclature is that of the Wisconsin State Laboratory of Hygiene]

Polycyclic aromatic hydrocarbon	Number of observations	Number of detections	Minimum (µg/L)	Maximum (µg/L)	Median (µg/L)	Mean (µg/L)	Standard deviation	Coefficient of variation
Acenaphthene	11	2	<0.064	0.16	<0.064	—	—	—
Acenaphthylene	11	0	<0.11	<0.11	<0.11	—	—	—
Anthracene	11	7	<0.031	0.56	0.05	0.15	0.19	1.27
Benzo (A) Anthracene	11	9	<0.093	4.00	0.25	0.94	1.35	1.43
Benzo (A) Pyrene	10	10	0.17	6.80	0.52	1.80	2.34	1.30
Benzo (B) Fluoranthene	11	11	0.24	12.00	0.67	2.64	3.82	1.45
Benzo (G,H,I,) Perylene	11	11	0.27	7.70	0.56	2.00	2.59	1.30
Benzo (K) Fluoranthene	11	10	<0.12	4.80	0.30	1.15	1.59	1.39
Chrysene	11	11	0.20	9.10	0.54	2.10	2.97	1.42
Dibenzo (A, H) Anthracene	11	0	<0.06	<0.06	<0.06	—	—	—
Fluoranthene	11	11	0.49	22.00	1.20	4.83	7.07	1.47
Fluorene	11	0	<0.52	<0.52	<0.52	—	—	—
Indeno (1.2.3-C,D) Pyrene	11	11	0.23	7.30	0.51	1.84	2.46	1.34
1-Methylnaphthalene	11	0	<0.064	<0.064	<0.064	—	—	—
2-Methylnaphthalene	11	0	<0.049	<0.049	<0.049	—	—	—
Naphthalene	11	2	<0.042	0.05	<0.042	—	—	—
Phenanthrene	11	11	0.12	8.50	0.41	1.74	2.72	1.56
Pyrene	11	11	0.33	16.00	0.87	3.51	5.17	1.48
Total PAH	11	11	2.05	98.96	5.72	22.52	32.27	1.43

Table 3E. Summary statistics of polycyclic aromatic hydrocarbons for commercial roof.

[<, less than; —, not determined; µg/L, micrograms per liter; chemical nomenclature is that of the Wisconsin State Laboratory of Hygiene]

Polycyclic aromatic hydrocarbon	Number of observations	Number of detections	Minimum (µg/L)	Maximum (µg/L)	Median (µg/L)	Mean (µg/L)	Standard deviation	Coefficient of variation
Acenaphthene	9	0	<0.064	<0.064	<0.064	—	—	—
Acenaphthylene	9	0	<0.11	<0.11	<0.11	—	—	—
Anthracene	9	1	<0.031	0.09	<0.031	—	—	—
Benzo (A) Anthracene	9	5	<0.093	0.58	0.10	0.16	0.16	0.99
Benzo (A) Pyrene	9	8	0.18	0.99	0.21	0.30	0.26	0.88
Benzo (B) Fluoranthene	9	8	0.20	1.30	0.24	0.36	0.36	0.99
Benzo (G,H,I,) Perylene	9	8	0.17	1.10	0.24	0.33	0.30	0.90
Benzo (K) Fluoranthene	9	2	<0.12	0.62	<0.12	—	—	—
Chrysene	9	8	0.15	1.10	0.19	0.29	0.31	1.09
Dibenzo (A, H) Anthracene	9	0	<0.06	<0.06	<0.06	—	—	—
Fluoranthene	9	9	0.12	2.90	0.53	0.76	0.82	1.08
Fluorene	9	0	<0.52	<0.52	<0.52	—	—	—
Indeno (1.2.3-C,D) Pyrene	9	7	0.17	1.00	0.21	0.29	0.28	0.97
1-Methylnaphthalene	9	0	<0.064	<0.064	<0.064	<0.064	—	—
2-Methylnaphthalene	9	0	<0.049	<0.049	<0.049	<0.049	—	—
Naphthalene	9	0	<0.042	<0.042	<0.042	<0.042	—	—
Phenanthrene	9	8	0.15	1.60	0.28	0.39	0.46	1.16
Pyrene	9	8	0.31	2.30	0.42	0.60	0.65	1.08
Total PAH	9	9	0.12	13.58	2.40	3.44	3.92	1.14

Table 3*F.* Summary statistics of polycyclic aromatic hydrocarbons for the mixed-use area (strip mall).

[<, less than; —, not determined; µg/L, micrograms per liter; chemical nomenclature is that of the Wisconsin State Laboratory of Hygiene]

Polycyclic aromatic hydrocarbon	Number of observations	Number of detections	Minimum (µg/L)	Maximum (µg/L)	Median (µg/L)	Mean (µg/L)	Standard deviation	Coefficient of variation
Acenaphthene	19	0	<0.064	<0.064	<0.064	—	—	—
Acenaphthylene	19	0	<0.11	<0.11	<0.11	—	—	—
Anthracene	19	0	<0.031	<0.031	<0.031	—	—	—
Benzo (A) Anthracene	19	19	0.09	0.47	0.15	0.22	0.14	0.64
Benzo (A) Pyrene	19	15	<0.16	1.20	0.32	0.46	0.33	0.72
Benzo (B) Fluoranthene	19	18	<0.13	1.70	0.60	0.74	0.53	0.72
Benzo (G,H,I,) Perylene	19	17	<0.14	1.70	0.56	0.69	0.48	0.70
Benzo (K) Fluoranthene	19	13	<0.12	0.53	0.21	0.26	0.16	0.60
Chrysene	19	19	0.04	1.40	0.52	0.59	0.42	0.71
Dibenzo (A, H) Anthracene	19	0	<0.034	<0.034	<0.034	—	—	—
Fluoranthene	19	18	<0.11	3.70	1.20	1.42	1.12	0.79
Fluorene	19	0	<0.52	<0.52	<0.52	—	—	—
Indeno (1.2.3-C,D) Pyrene	19	18	<0.095	1.50	0.55	0.65	0.45	0.69
1-Methylnaphthalene	19	0	<0.064	<0.064	<0.064	—	—	—
2-Methylnaphthalene	19	0	<0.049	<0.049	<0.049	—	—	—
Naphthalene	19	0	<0.042	<0.042	<0.042	—	—	—
Phenanthrene	19	13	<0.093	1.20	0.36	0.42	0.33	0.79
Pyrene	19	17	<0.11	2.20	0.82	0.92	0.74	0.80
Total PAH	19	19	0.14	14.77	5.72	6.21	4.75	0.76

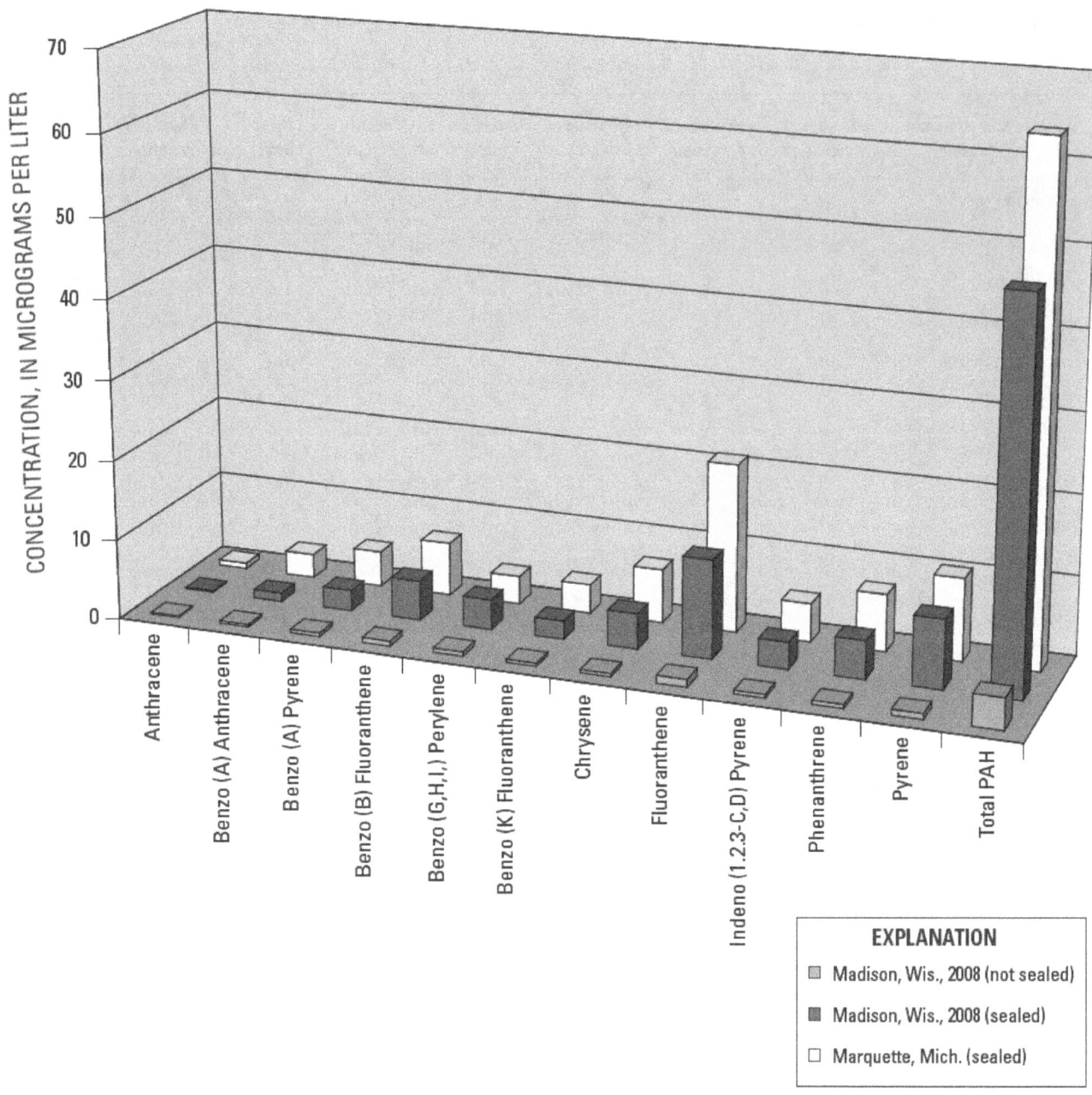

Figure 10A. Geometric mean concentrations of polycyclic aromatic hydrocarbons from parking lots in Madison, Wis., and Marquette, Mich.

Figures 10A through 10F compare geometric mean concentrations of select PAH compounds from this study to those from similar studies done in Marquette, Mich., and Madison, Wis. (Steuer and others, 1997) in 1993 and 1994, respectively. Source areas monitored as part of the Madison, Wis., study in 1994 included only feeder, collector, and arterial streets. In contrast to this study, Waschbusch and Steuer collected urban runoff with source-area-specific water-quality samplers rather than autosamplers placed at the basin outfall. Descriptions of each source-area sampler are detailed in Waschbusch (1999).

In general, the pattern of individual PAH compound concentrations were similar between studies for all source areas monitored. PAH concentrations for feeder-street runoff were similar in both Madison studies but tended to be lower in Marquette, Mich. (fig. 10C). Conversely, collector-street runoff had similar PAH concentrations for both Madison studies, but concentrations were higher in the Marquette runoff (fig. 10D). PAH concentrations for arterial street runoff were similar for all three studies (fig. 10E).

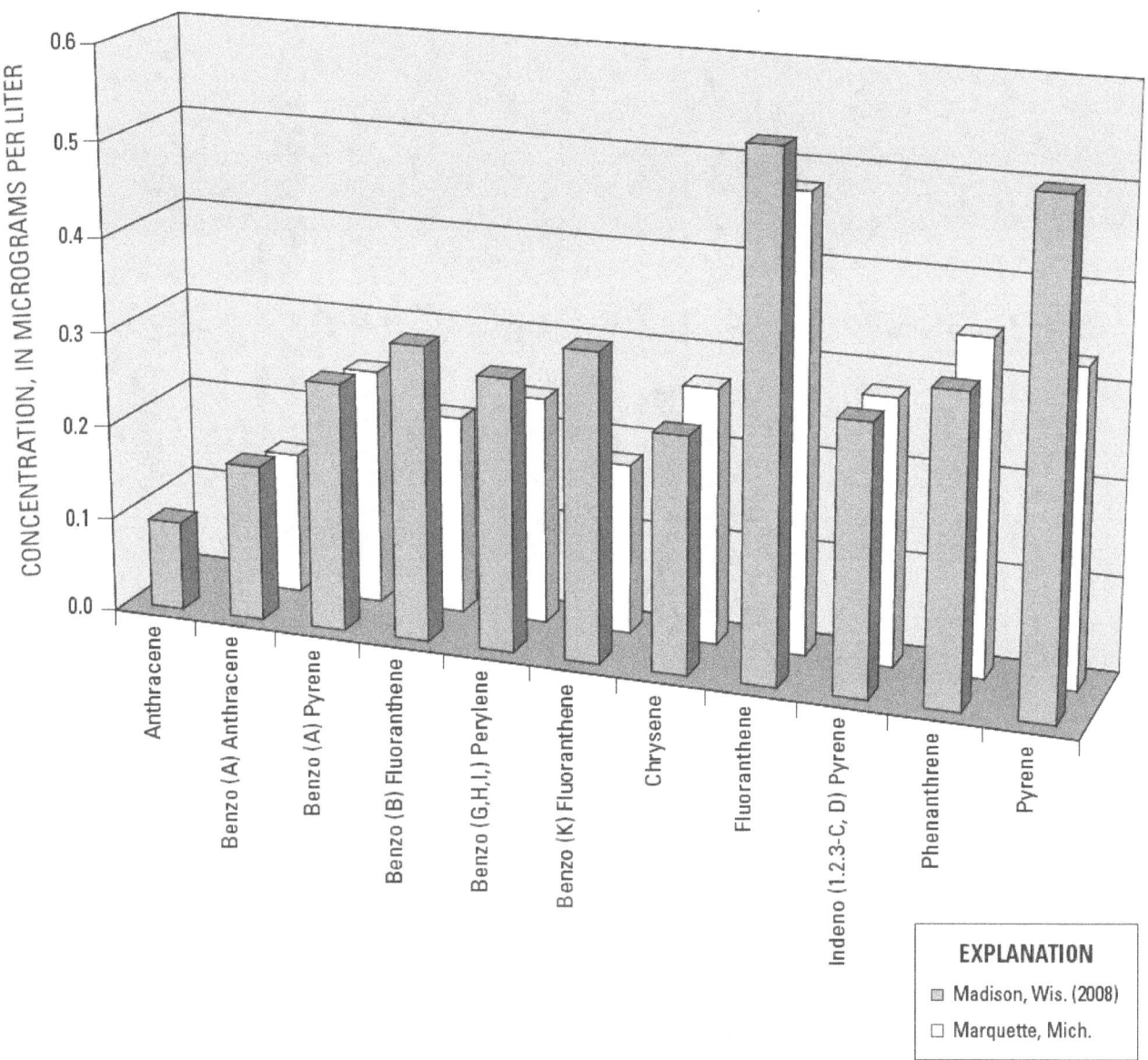

Figure 10B. Geometric mean concentrations of polycyclic aromatic hydrocarbons from commercial roofs in Madison, Wis., and Marquette, Mich.

Geometric mean concentrations for most individual PAH compounds were significantly greater for parking lots that were sealed than for those that were not sealed. Runoff from both of the coal-tar sealed parking lots that were monitored in Marquette, Mich., and Madison, Wis., had similar geometric mean concentrations despite the distance between locations and length of time between studies. These results are consistent with a similar study that examined PAH concentrations from coal-tar-sealed parking lots in Austin, Tex. (Van Metre and others, 2005).

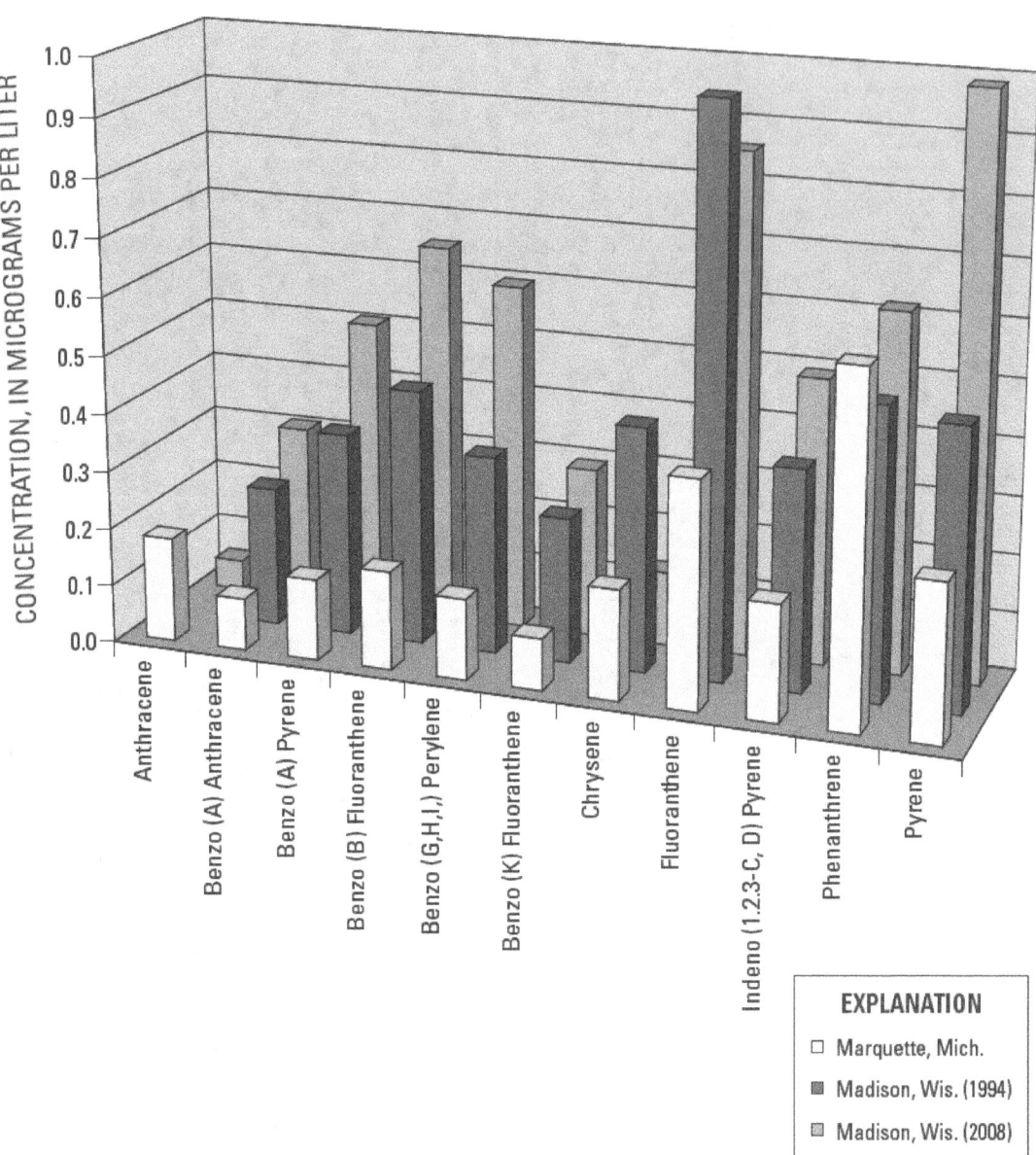

Figure 10C. Geometric mean concentrations of polycyclic aromatic hydrocarbons from feeder streets in Madison, Wis., and Marquette, Mich.

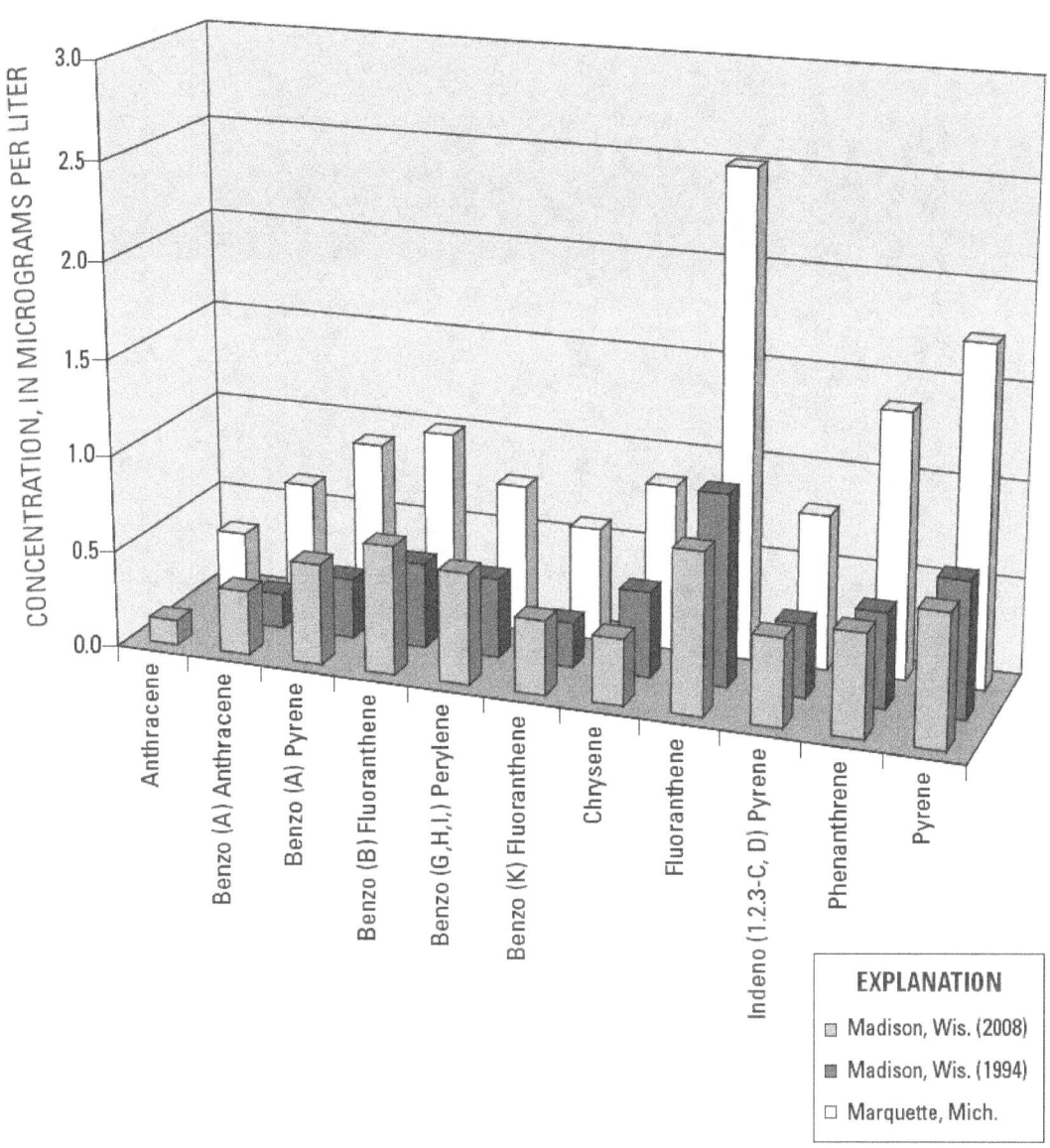

Figure 10D. Geometric mean concentrations of polycyclic aromatic hydrocarbons from collector streets in Madison, Wis., and Marquette, Mich.

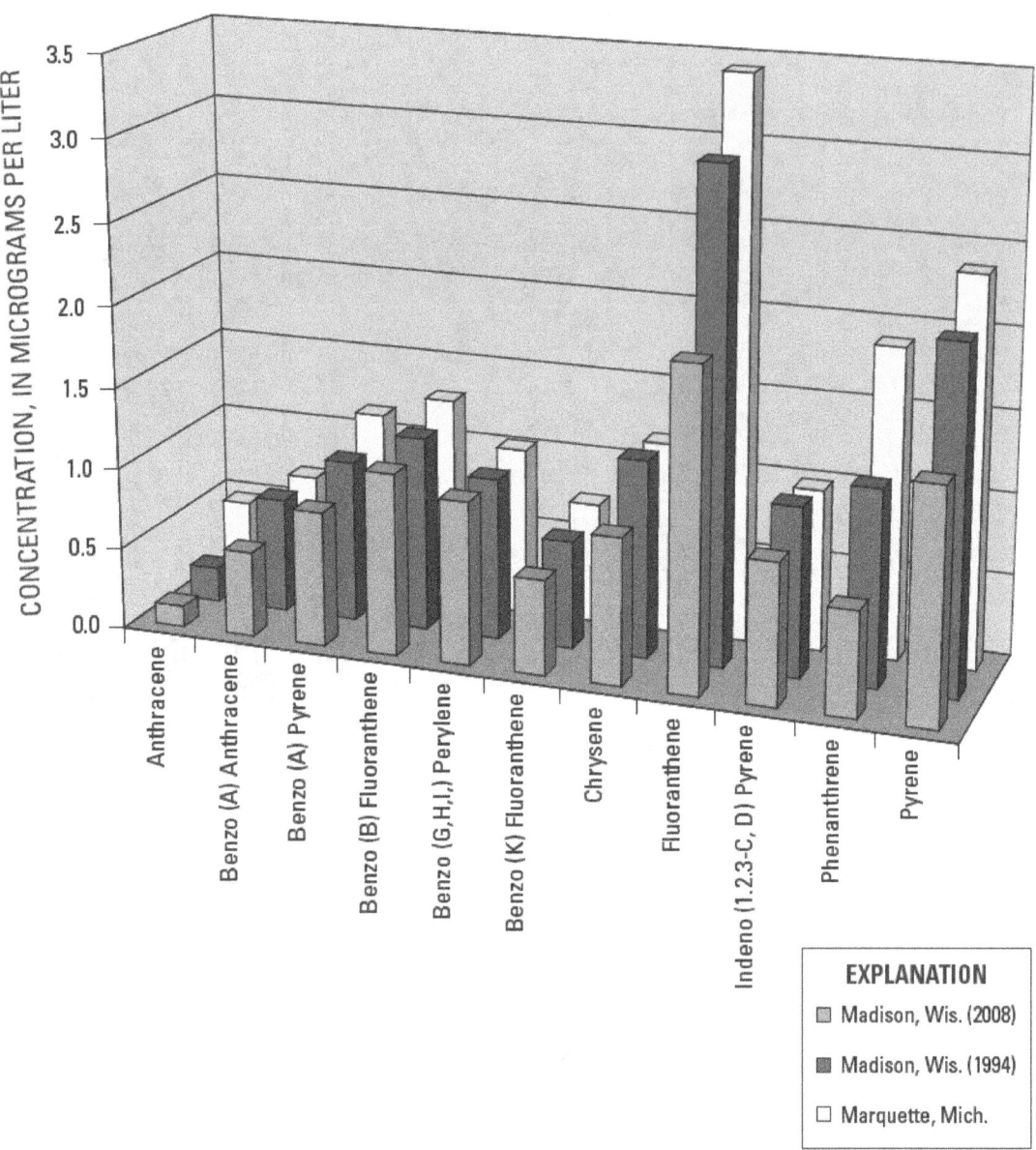

Figure 10*E*.   Geometric mean concentrations of polycyclic aromatic hydrocarbons from arterial streets in Madison, Wis., and Marquette, Mich.

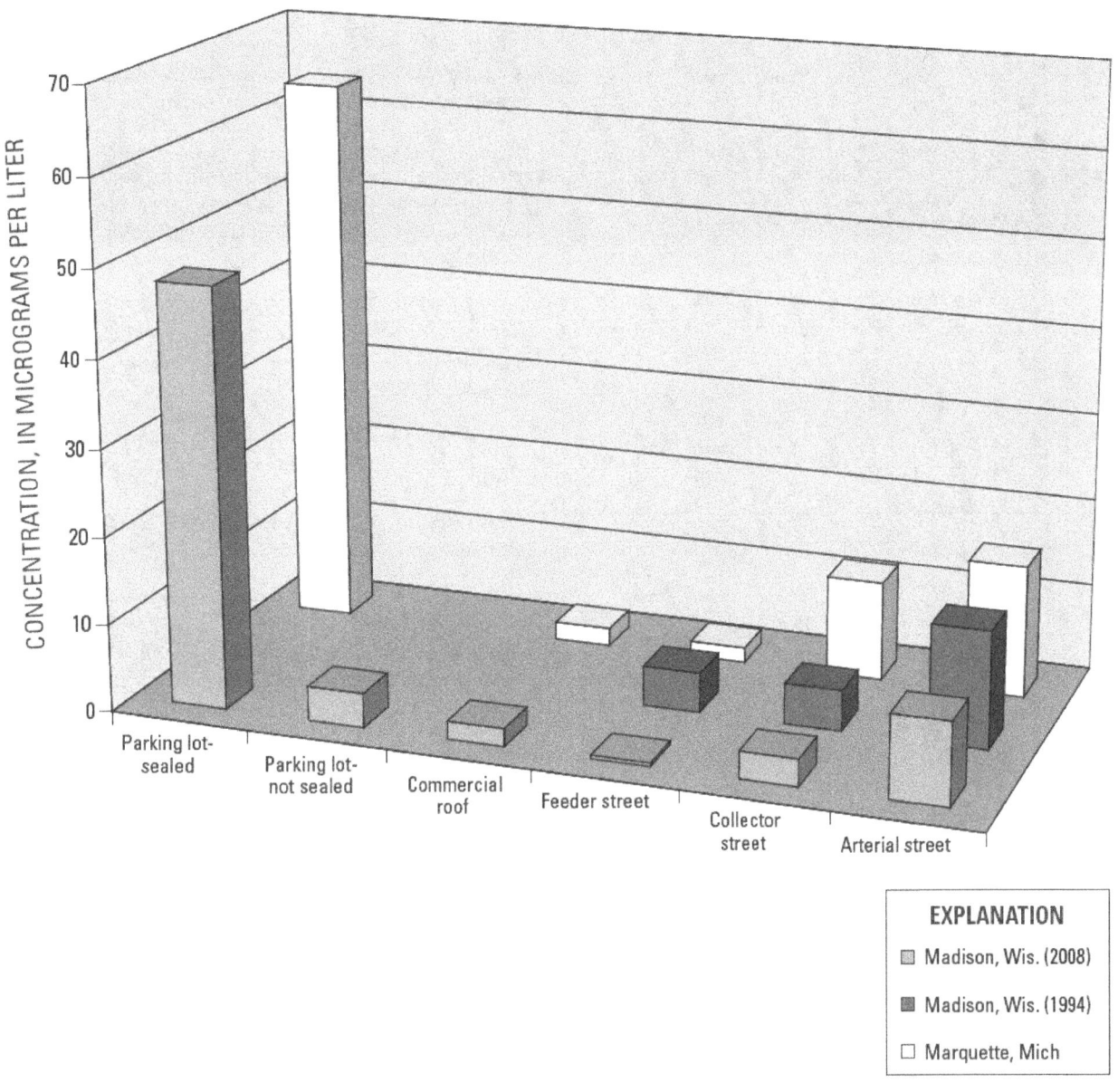

Figure 10F. Geometric mean concentrations of total polycyclic aromatic hydrocarbons from source areas monitored in Madison, Wis., and Marquette, Mich.

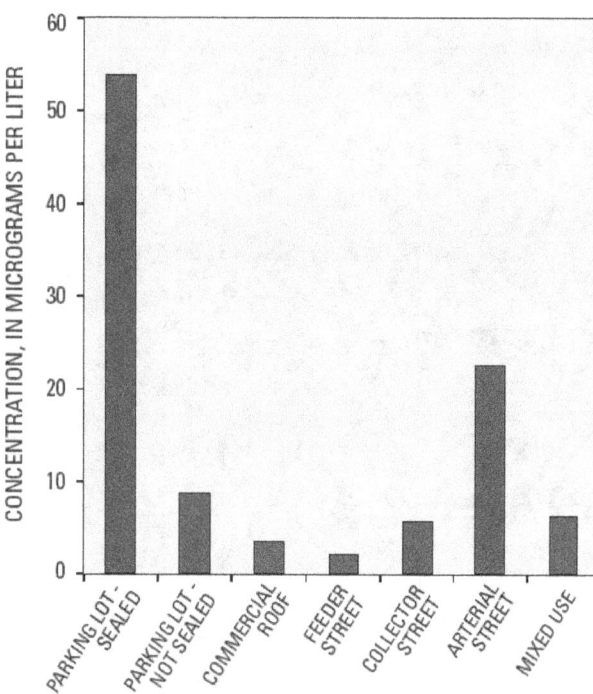

Figure 11. Mean concentration of total polycyclic aromatic hydrocarbons from source areas monitored in Madison, Wis. (2008).

Figure 11 shows the mean total PAH concentrations for the Madison, Wis., 2008 study. Runoff from the sealed parking lot had the largest concentration, followed by runoff from the unsealed parking lots, the arterial street, the mixed-use area (strip mall), the collector street, the commercial roof, and finally, the feeder street. Similar to the Madison 2008 study, geometric mean total PAH concentrations in the Marquette study were greatest for sealed parking lots followed by those for arterial, collector, and feeder streets (fig. 10F). Runoff from commercial roofs had the lowest total PAH geometric mean concentrations (fig. 10F).

References

Helsel, D.R., 2005, Nondetects and data analysis—Statistics for censored environmental data: Hoboken, N.J., John Wiley and Sons, 250 p.

Hoffman, E.J., 1985, Urban runoff pollutant inputs to Narragansett Bay—Comparison to point sources, *in* Proceedings from the Conference on Perspectives on Nonpoint Source Pollution: U.S. Environmental Protection Agency, EPA 440/5–85–001, p. 159–164.

Menzie, C.A., Hoeppner, S.S., Cura, J.J., Freshman, J.S., and LaFrey, E.N., 2002, Urban and suburban storm water runoff as a source of polycyclic aromatic hydrocarbons (PAHs) to Massachusetts estuarine and coastal environments: Estuaries, v. 25, no. 2, p. 165–176.

Stein, E.D., Tiefenthaler, L.L., and Schiff, K., 2006, Watershed-based sources of polycyclic aromatic hydrocarbons in urban storm water: Environmental Toxicology and Chemistry, v. 25, no. 2, p. 373–385.

Steuer, J.J., Selbig, W.R., and Hornewer, N.J., 1996, Contaminant concentration in stormwater from eight Lake Superior basin cities, 1993–94, U.S. Geological Survey Open-File Report 96–122, 16 p.

Steuer, J.J., Selbig, W.R., Hornewer, N.J., and Prey, Jeffrey, 1997, Sources of contamination in an urban basin in Marquette, Michigan and an analysis of concentrations, loads, and data quality: U.S. Geological Survey Water-Resources Investigations Report 97–4242, 25 p.

Van Metre, P.C.; Mahler, B.J.; Scoggins, Mateo; and Hamilton, P.A., 2005, Parking lot sealcoat—A major source of polycyclic aromatic hydrocarbons (PAHs) in urban and suburban environments: U.S. Geological Survey Fact Sheet 2005–3147, 4 p.

Waschbusch, R.J., Selbig, W.R., and Bannerman, R.T., 1999, Sources of phosphorus in stormwater and street dirt from two urban residential basins in Madison, Wisconsin, 1994–95, U.S. Geological Survey Water-Resources Investigations Report 99–4021, 47 p.

Prepared by the Wisconsin Water Science Center:

U.S. Geological Survey
Wisconsin Water Science Center
8505 Research Way
Middleton, WI 53562
tel: (608) 828-9901
fax: (608) 821-3817

This publication is available online at URL
http://pubs.usgs.gov/ofr/2009/1077

Information regarding the Wisconsin Water Science Center is available at URL: http://wi.water.usgs.gov

Information regarding the Wisconsin Water Science Center's Lakes Team is available at URL: http://wi.water.usgs.gov/lakes

Appendix Tables 1–1 – 1–7

Table 1–1.   Concentrations of PAH compounds and total PAH summation for parking lots 1 and 2.

[<, less than; all values expressed as micrograms per liter; chemical nomenclature is that of the Wisconsin State Laboratory of Hygiene]

Sample ID	Date	Acenaphthene	Acenaphthylene	Anthracene	Benzo (A) Anthracene	Benzo (A) Pyrene	Benzo (B) Fluoranthene	Benzo (G,H,I,) Perylene	Benzo (K) Fluoranthene	Chrysene	Dibenzo (A, H) Anthracene
PARKING LOT 1 - 1	09/10/2006	<.064	<.11	<.031	<.093	<.16	<.13	<.14	<.12	0.04	<.034
PARKING LOT 1 - 2	10/10/2006	<.064	<.11	<.031	<.093	<.16	0.19	0.21	<.12	0.14	<.034
PARKING LOT 1 - 3	10/16/2006	0.20	<.11	<.031	<.093	0.22	0.29	0.32	<.12	0.21	<.034
PARKING LOT 1 - 4	10/21/2006	<.064	<.11	<.031	<.093	0.26	0.36	0.38	0.16	0.28	<.034
PARKING LOT 1 - 5	04/02/2007	<.064	<.11	0.19	0.75	1.20	1.80	1.60	0.81	1.50	<0.15
PARKING LOT 1 - 6	04/24/2007	<.064	<.11	<.031	0.22	0.40	0.67	0.59	0.30	0.55	<0.064
PARKING LOT 1 - 7	04/25/2007	<.064	<.11	0.05	0.31	0.57	0.98	0.85	0.45	0.79	0.10
PARKING LOT 1 - 8	05/24/2007	<.064	<.11	<0.040	0.31	0.67	1.30	1.10	0.56	0.98	<0.088
PARKING LOT 1 - 9	06/18/2007	<.064	<.11	<.031	<.093	0.26	0.44	0.43	0.18	0.31	<.034
PARKING LOT 1 - 10	07/26/2007	<.064	<.11	<.031	0.25	0.37	1.30	1.10	0.51	0.87	<0.093
PARKING LOT 1 - 11	08/04/2007	<.064	<.11	<.031	<.093	<.16	0.14	0.16	<.12	0.10	<.034
PARKING LOT 1 - 12	08/06/2007	<.064	<.11	<.031	<.093	<.16	<.13	0.14	<.12	0.08	<.034
PARKING LOT 1 - 13	08/15/2007	<.064	<.11	<.031	<.093	<.16	0.21	0.23	<.12	0.13	<.034

Table 1–1. Concentrations of PAH compounds and total PAH summation for parking lots 1 and 2—Continued.

[<, less than; all values expressed as micrograms per liter; chemical nomenclature is that of the Wisconsin State Laboratory of Hygiene]

Sample ID	Date	Fluoran-thene	Fluorene	Indeno (1.2.3-C,D) Pyrene	1-Methyl-naphthalene	2-Methyl-naphthalene	Naphthalene	Phenan-threne	Pyrene	Total PAH
PARKING LOT 1 - 1	09/10/2006	<.11	<.52	<.093	<.064	<.049	<.042	<.093	<.11	0.04
PARKING LOT 1 - 2	10/10/2006	0.27	<.52	0.15	<.064	<.049	<.042	<.093	0.20	1.16
PARKING LOT 1 - 3	10/16/2006	0.42	<.52	0.25	<.064	<.049	<.042	0.21	0.32	2.44
PARKING LOT 1 - 4	10/21/2006	0.52	<.52	0.28	<.064	<.049	<.042	0.14	0.40	2.78
PARKING LOT 1 - 5	04/02/2007	3.60	<.52	1.40	<.064	<.049	<.042	1.80	2.70	17.35
PARKING LOT 1 - 6	04/24/2007	1.40	<.52	0.44	<.064	<.049	<.042	0.37	0.94	5.88
PARKING LOT 1 - 7	04/25/2007	1.90	<.52	0.64	<.064	<.049	<.042	0.71	1.40	8.75
PARKING LOT 1 - 8	05/24/2007	2.20	<.52	0.93	<.064	<.049	<.042	0.81	1.50	10.36
PARKING LOT 1 - 9	06/18/2007	0.60	<.52	0.33	<.064	<.049	<.042	0.18	0.42	3.15
PARKING LOT 1 - 10	07/26/2007	1.70	<.52	0.91	<.064	<.049	<.042	0.57	1.30	8.88
PARKING LOT 1 - 11	08/04/2007	0.18	<.52	0.15	<.064	<.049	<.042	<.093	0.13	0.86
PARKING LOT 1 - 12	08/06/2007	0.16	<.52	0.12	<.064	<.049	<.042	<.093	0.12	0.62
PARKING LOT 1 - 13	08/15/2007	0.25	<.52	0.18	<.064	<.049	<.042	<.093	0.20	1.20

Table 1–1. Concentrations of PAH compounds and total PAH summation for parking lots 1 and 2—Continued.

[<, less than; all values expressed as micrograms per liter; chemical nomenclature is that of the Wisconsin State Laboratory of Hygiene]

Sample ID	Date	Acenaphthene	Acenaphthylene	Anthracene	Benzo (A) Anthracene	Benzo (A) Pyrene	Benzo (B) Fluoranthene	Benzo (G,H,I.) Perylene	Benzo (K) Fluoranthene	Chrysene	Dibenzo (A, H) Anthracene
PARKING LOT 1 - 14	08/18/2007	<.064	<.11	<.031	0.25	0.50	0.83	0.80	0.37	0.59	<0.071
PARKING LOT 1 - 15	09/21/2007	<.064	<.11	<.031	0.18	0.36	0.64	0.67	0.28	0.46	<0.059
PARKING LOT 2 - 1	08/23/2006	0.30	<.11	1.30	3.60	5.00	6.10	5.00	2.90	5.70	<0.50
PARKING LOT 2 - 2	09/10/2006	<.064	<.11	<.031	<.093	0.16	0.22	0.23	<.12	0.17	<0.034
PARKING LOT 2 - 3	10/04/2006	<.064	<.11	0.05	0.33	1.00	1.70	1.30	0.77	1.50	<0.12
PARKING LOT 2 - 4	10/16/2006	<.064	<.11	<.031	<.093	0.16	0.17	0.18	<.12	0.12	<0.034
PARKING LOT 2 - 5	03/10/2007	<.064	<.11	<.031	0.17	0.45	0.69	0.60	0.31	0.57	<0.050
PARKING LOT 2 - 6	03/11/2007	<.064	<.11	<.031	0.16	0.35	0.53	0.46	0.24	0.42	<0.036
PARKING LOT 2 - 7	03/12/2007	<.064	<.11	<.031	0.17	0.34	0.54	0.46	0.23	0.43	<0.038
PARKING LOT 2 - 8	03/13/2007	<.064	<.11	<.031	0.24	0.47	0.81	0.68	0.33	0.65	<0.057
PARKING LOT 2 - 9	03/31/2007	<.064	<.11	0.19	1.20	2.00	2.90	2.50	1.40	2.50	<0.23
PARKING LOT 2 - 10	04/03/2007	<.064	<.11	0.07	0.48	0.82	1.20	1.00	0.54	0.98	<0.098
PARKING LOT 2 - 11	04/24/2007	<.064	<.11	<.031	<.093	0.18	0.41	0.35	0.17	0.30	<.034
PARKING LOT 2 - 12	05/24/2007	<.064	<.11	<.031	0.11	0.25	0.44	0.41	0.20	0.34	<.034

Table 1–1. Concentrations of PAH compounds and total PAH summation for parking lots 1 and 2—Continued.

[<, less than; all values expressed as micrograms per liter; chemical nomenclature is that of the Wisconsin State Laboratory of Hygiene]

Sample ID	Date	Fluoran-thene	Fluorene	Indeno (1,2,3-C,D) Pyrene	1-Methyl-naphthalene	2-Methyl-naphthalene	Naphthalene	Phenan-threne	Pyrene	Total PAH
PARKING LOT 1 - 14	08/18/2007	1.10	<.52	0.65	<.064	<.049	<.042	0.36	0.88	6.33
PARKING LOT 1 - 15	09/21/2007	0.88	<.52	0.52	<.064	<.049	<.042	0.31	0.68	4.98
PARKING LOT 2 - 1	08/23/2006	16.00	0.65	4.00	<.064	<.049	<.042	8.70	12.00	71.25
PARKING LOT 2 - 2	09/10/2006	0.29	<.52	0.18	<.064	<.049	<.042	<.093	0.22	1.47
PARKING LOT 2 - 3	10/04/2006	3.50	<.52	1.30	<.064	<.049	<.042	1.20	2.60	15.25
PARKING LOT 2 - 4	10/16/2006	0.24	<.52	0.13	<.064	<.049	<.042	<.093	0.22	1.22
PARKING LOT 2 - 5	03/10/2007	1.40	<.52	0.54	<.064	<.049	<.042	0.39	1.00	6.12
PARKING LOT 2 - 6	03/11/2007	1.00	<.52	0.41	<.064	<.049	<.042	0.24	0.75	4.56
PARKING LOT 2 - 7	03/12/2007	1.10	<.52	0.39	<.064	<.049	<.042	0.32	0.78	4.76
PARKING LOT 2 - 8	03/13/2007	1.60	<.52	0.61	<.064	<.049	<.042	0.45	1.20	7.04
PARKING LOT 2 - 9	03/31/2007	6.10	<.52	2.20	<.064	<.049	<.042	2.50	4.50	27.99
PARKING LOT 2 - 10	04/03/2007	2.50	<.52	0.93	<.064	<.049	<.042	1.20	1.80	11.52
PARKING LOT 2 - 11	04/24/2007	0.65	<.52	0.28	<.064	<.049	<.042	0.20	0.43	2.97
PARKING LOT 2 - 12	05/24/2007	0.77	<.52	0.32	<.064	<.049	<.042	0.31	0.54	3.69

Table 1–2. Concentrations of PAH compounds and total PAH summation for parking lot 3.

[<, less than; —, data not available; all values expressed as micrograms per liter; chemical nomenclature is that of the Wisconsin State Laboratory of Hygiene]

Sample ID	Date	Acenaphthene	Acenaphthylene	Anthracene	Benzo (A) Anthracene	Benzo (A) Pyrene	Benzo (B) Fluoranthene	Benzo (G,H,I,) Perylene	Benzo (K) Fluoranthene	Chrysene	Dibenzo (A, H) Anthracene
PARKING LOT 3 - 1	04/29/2006	0.08	<.11	0.25	1.20	2.80	5.20	4.00	2.40	4.60	<.37
PARKING LOT 3 - 2	05/11/2006	<.064	<.11	0.05	0.17	0.66	1.70	1.20	0.68	1.40	<.12
PARKING LOT 3 - 3	06/10/2006	<.064	<.11	0.19	<.59	—	4.00	3.00	1.70	3.60	<.28
PARKING LOT 3 - 4	06/25/2006	0.16	<.11	—	<1.0	1.90	5.20	4.10	2.30	4.80	<.36
PARKING LOT 3 - 5	07/11/2006	<.064	<.11	0.14	<.57	0.78	3.40	2.60	1.50	3.10	<.23
PARKING LOT 3 - 6	07/20/2006	0.09	<.11	—	1.90	—	7.50	5.70	3.60	7.00	<.53
PARKING LOT 3 - 7	07/27/2006	0.09	<.11	0.30	2.00	3.80	5.80	4.80	2.70	5.20	<.47
PARKING LOT 3 - 8	08/23/2006	<.064	<.11	0.30	1.80	5.50	8.10	6.30	3.70	7.10	<.60
PARKING LOT 3 - 9	08/24/2006	<.064	<.11	0.24	1.50	3.90	5.40	4.30	2.50	4.70	<.45
PARKING LOT 3 - 10	08/25/2006	<.064	<.11	0.29	1.70	3.60	4.80	3.80	2.20	4.30	<.42
PARKING LOT 3 - 11	04/23/2007	—	<.11	0.35	1.70	5.70	9.80	7.10	4.60	8.40	<.79
PARKING LOT 3 - 12	04/24/2007	<.064	<.11	0.06	0.34	0.84	2.10	1.40	1.10	1.80	<.14

Table 1–2. Concentrations of PAH compounds and total PAH summation for parking lot 3—Continued.

[<, less than; —, data not available; all values expressed as micrograms per liter; chemical nomenclature is that of the Wisconsin State Laboratory of Hygiene]

Sample ID	Date	Fluoran-thene	Fluorene	Indeno (1,2,3-C,D) Pyrene	1-Methyl-naphthalene	2-Methyl-naphthalene	Naphthalene	Phenan-threne	Pyrene	Total PAH
PARKING LOT 3 - 1	04/29/2006	13.00	<.52	3.80	<.064	<.049	<.042	5.80	9.20	52.33
PARKING LOT 3 - 2	05/11/2006	3.70	<.52	1.10	<.064	<.049	<.042	1.40	2.50	14.56
PARKING LOT 3 - 3	06/10/2006	11.00	<.52	2.80	<.064	<.049	<.042	4.10	7.10	37.49
PARKING LOT 3 - 4	06/25/2006	15.00	<.52	3.80	<.064	<.049	<.042	7.30	10.00	54.56
PARKING LOT 3 - 5	07/11/2006	8.90	<.52	2.40	<.064	<.049	<.042	3.20	5.90	31.92
PARKING LOT 3 - 6	07/20/2006	19.00	<.52	5.30	<.064	<.049	<.042	7.20	14.00	71.29
PARKING LOT 3 - 7	07/27/2006	13.00	<.52	4.30	<.064	<.049	<.042	5.20	10.00	57.19
PARKING LOT 3 - 8	08/23/2006	18.00	<.52	5.90	<.064	<.049	<.042	6.30	13.00	76.00
PARKING LOT 3 - 9	08/24/2006	12.00	<.52	4.10	<.064	<.049	<.042	4.20	9.00	51.84
PARKING LOT 3 - 10	08/25/2006	11.00	<.52	3.50	<.064	<.049	<.042	4.00	8.70	47.89
PARKING LOT 3 - 11	04/23/2007	24.00	<.52	5.80	<.064	0.11	<.042	11.00	17.00	95.56
PARKING LOT 3 - 12	04/24/2007	4.50	<.52	1.20	<.064	<.049	<.042	1.90	3.10	18.34

Table 1–2.   Concentrations of PAH compounds and total PAH summation for parking lot 3—Continued.

[<, less than; —, data not available; all values expressed as micrograms per liter; chemical nomenclature is that of the Wisconsin State Laboratory of Hygiene]

Sample ID	Date	Acenaphthene	Acenaphthylene	Anthracene	Benzo (A) Anthracene	Benzo (A) Pyrene	Benzo (B) Fluoranthene	Benzo (G,H,I,) Perylene	Benzo (K) Fluoranthene	Chrysene	Dibenzo (A, H) Anthracene
PARKING LOT 3 - 13	05/15/2007	0.17	<.11	0.25	1.10	3.70	6.40	4.40	2.80	5.50	0.47
PARKING LOT 3 - 14	05/24/2007	<.064	<.11	<.28	—	6.10	10.00	7.40	4.80	8.80	<.58
PARKING LOT 3 - 15	07/03/2007	0.11	<.11	0.25	0.97	2.40	3.80	2.80	1.80	3.60	<.22

Table 1–2.   Concentrations of PAH compounds and total PAH summation for parking lot 3—Continued.

[<, less than; —, data not available; all values expressed as micrograms per liter; chemical nomenclature is that of the Wisconsin State Laboratory of Hygiene]

Sample ID	Date	Fluoranthene	Fluorene	Indeno (1,2,3-C,D) Pyrene	1-Methyl-naphthalene	2-Methyl-naphthalene	Naphthalene	Phenanthrene	Pyrene	Total PAH
PARKING LOT 3 - 13	05/15/2007	18.00	<.52	3.60	<.064	0.09	<.042	6.60	11.00	64.08
PARKING LOT 3 - 14	05/24/2007	25.00	<.52	6.20	<.064	0.09	<.042	8.80	17.00	94.19
PARKING LOT 3 - 15	07/03/2007	11.00	<.52	2.40	<.064	0.09	<.042	4.10	7.30	40.62

Table 1–3. Concentrations of PAH compounds and total PAH summation for feeder street.

[<, less than; —, data not available; all values expressed as micrograms per liter; chemical nomenclature is that of the Wisconsin State Laboratory of Hygiene]

Sample ID	Date	Acenaph-thene	Acenaph-thylene	Anthracene	Benzo (A) Anthracene	Benzo (A) Pyrene	Benzo (B) Fluoran-thene	Benzo (G,H,I,) Perylene	Benzo (K) Fluoran-thene	Chrysene	Dibenzo (A, H) Anthra-cene
FEEDER - 1	08/14/2007	<.064	<.11	<.031	<.093	<.16	<.13	<.14	<.12	0.04	<.034
FEEDER - 2	08/18/2007	<.064	<.11	<.031	<.093	<.16	<.13	<.14	<.12	0.03	<.034
FEEDER - 3	09/06/2007	<.064	<.11	<.031	<.093	<.16	<.13	<.14	<.12	0.06	<.034
FEEDER - 4	09/21/2007	<.064	<.11	<.031	<.093	<.16	<.13	—	<.12	0.08	<.034
FEEDER - 5	09/25/2007	<.064	<.11	<.031	<.093	<.16	<.13	<.14	<.12	0.05	<.034
FEEDER - 6	10/02/2007	<.064	<.11	<.031	<.093	<.16	<.13	<.14	<.12	<.027	<.034
FEEDER - 7	10/15/2007	<.064	<.11	<.031	<.093	<.16	<.13	<.14	<.12	<.027	<.034
FEEDER - 8	10/17/2007	<.064	<.11	<.031	<.093	<.16	<.13	<.14	<.12	<.027	<.034
FEEDER - 9	04/10/2008	<.064	<.11	0.05	0.30	0.50	0.65	0.57	0.32	0.53	<.080
FEEDER - 10	04/24/2008	<.064	<.11	<.15	0.58	0.85	1.30	1.10	0.40	1.00	<.16
FEEDER - 11	05/02/2008	<.064	<.11	<.045	0.28	0.45	0.65	0.59	0.24	0.55	<.080
FEEDER - 12	05/06/2008	<.064	<.11	<.031	<.093	<.16	<.13	<.14	<.12	0.04	<.034
FEEDER - 13	05/29/2008	<.064	<.11	<.031	<.093	<.16	<.13	<.14	<.12	0.06	<.034
FEEDER - 14	06/05/2008	<.064	<.11	<.031	0.40	0.70	0.80	0.82	0.24	0.73	<.12
FEEDER - 15	06/12/2008	<.064	<.11	<.031	0.14	0.25	0.27	0.25	<.12	0.19	<.035

Table 1–3. Concentrations of PAH compounds and total PAH summation for feeder street—Continued.

[<, less than; —, data not available; all values expressed as micrograms per liter; chemical nomenclature is that of the Wisconsin State Laboratory of Hygiene]

Sample ID	Date	Fluoran- thene	Fluorene	Indeno (1,2,3-C,D) Pyrene	1-Methyl- naphthalene	2-Methyl- naphthalene	Naphthalene	Phenan- threne	Pyrene	Total PAH
FEEDER - 1	08/14/2007	<.11	<.52	<.093	<.1	<.049	<.042	<.093	<.11	0.04
FEEDER - 2	08/18/2007	<.11	<.52	<.093	<.1	<.049	<.042	<.093	<.11	0.03
FEEDER - 3	09/06/2007	—	<.52	<.093	<.1	<.049	<.042	<.093	—	0.06
FEEDER - 4	09/21/2007	—	<.52	<.14	<.1	<.049	<.042	<.093	—	0.08
FEEDER - 5	09/25/2007	<.11	<.52	<.093	<.1	<.049	<.042	<.093	<.11	0.05
FEEDER - 6	10/02/2007	<.11	<.52	<.093	<.1	<.049	<.042	<.093	<.11	—
FEEDER - 7	10/15/2007	<.11	<.52	<.093	<.1	<.049	<.042	<.093	<.11	—
FEEDER - 8	10/17/2007	<.11	<.52	<.093	<.1	<.049	<.042	<.093	<.11	—
FEEDER - 9	04/10/2008	1.40	<.52	0.47	<.064	<.049	<.042	0.62	1.00	6.41
FEEDER - 10	04/24/2008	2.70	<.52	<1.2	<.064	<.049	<.042	1.30	1.90	11.13
FEEDER - 11	05/02/2008	1.20	<.52	0.56	<.064	<.049	<.042	0.51	0.91	5.94
FEEDER - 12	05/06/2008	<.11	<.52	<.093	<.064	<.049	<.042	<.093	<.11	0.04
FEEDER - 13	05/29/2008	0.12	<.52	<.15	<.064	<.049	<.042	<.093	<.11	0.18
FEEDER - 14	06/05/2008	1.60	<.52	0.86	<.064	<.049	<.042	0.99	1.40	8.54
FEEDER - 15	06/12/2008	0.46	<.52	0.26	<.064	<.049	<.042	0.22	0.39	2.43

Table 1-4. Concentrations of PAH compounds and total PAH summation for collector street.

[<, less than; —, data not available; all values expressed as micrograms per liter; chemical nomenclature is that of the Wisconsin State Laboratory of Hygiene]

Sample ID	Date	Acenaphthene	Acenaphthylene	Anthracene	Benzo (A) Anthracene	Benzo (A) Pyrene	Benzo (B) Fluoranthene	Benzo (G.H.I.) Perylene	Benzo (K) Fluoranthene	Chrysene	Dibenzo (A, H) Anthracene
COLLECTOR - 1	07/26/2007	<.064	<.11	<.031	<.093	<.16	<.13	<.14	<.12	0.11	<.034
COLLECTOR - 2	08/04/2007	<.064	<.11	<.031	<.093	<.16	<.13	<.14	<.12	<.027	<.034
COLLECTOR - 3	08/14/2007	<.064	<.11	<.031	0.21	0.31	0.43	0.36	0.21	0.39	<0.049
COLLECTOR - 4	08/18/2007	<.064	<.11	0.07	0.29	0.36	0.42	0.38	0.20	0.39	<0.055
COLLECTOR - 5	08/22/2007	<.064	<.11	<.031	<.093	<.16	0.29	0.26	<.12	0.22	<0.035
COLLECTOR - 6	08/27/2007	<.064	<.11	<.031	<.093	<.16	<.13	<.14	<.12	0.09	<.034
COLLECTOR - 7	09/21/2007	<.064	<.11	<.031	0.29	0.40	0.50	0.46	0.26	0.46	<0.056
COLLECTOR - 8	10/02/2007	<.064	<.11	<.031	0.14	0.22	0.32	0.30	<.12	0.27	<0.043
COLLECTOR - 9	10/15/2007	<.064	<.11	<.031	<.093	<.16	<.13	<.14	<.12	0.06	<.034
COLLECTOR - 10	10/17/2007	<.064	<.11	<.031	<.093	<.16	<.13	<.14	<.12	0.08	<.034
COLLECTOR - 11	03/31/2008	0.12	<.11	0.42	1.60	2.90	4.50	3.60	2.10	3.70	<.50
COLLECTOR - 12	04/08/2008	<.064	<.11	<.031	0.13	0.29	0.56	0.47	0.24	0.41	<.071
COLLECTOR - 13	04/10/2008	<.064	<.11	0.08	0.41	0.64	0.99	0.83	0.47	0.81	<.13
COLLECTOR - 14	04/24/2008	0.22	<.11	<.50	2.20	2.90	3.40	2.60	1.30	2.90	<.36

Table 1–4.   Concentrations of PAH compounds and total PAH summation for collector street—Continued.

[<, less than; —, data not available; all values expressed as micrograms per liter; chemical nomenclature is that of the Wisconsin State Laboratory of Hygiene]

Sample ID	Date	Fluoran-thene	Fluorene	Indeno (1,2,3-C,D) Pyrene	1-Methyl-naphthalene	2-Methyl-naphthalene	Naphthalene	Phenan-threne	Pyrene	Total PAH
COLLECTOR - 1	07/26/2007	0.25	<.52	<.093	<.064	<.049	<.042	<.093	0.15	0.51
COLLECTOR - 2	08/04/2007	<.11	<.52	<.093	<.064	<.049	<.042	<.093	<.11	—
COLLECTOR - 3	08/14/2007	0.93	<.52	0.31	<.064	<.049	<.042	0.33	0.69	4.17
COLLECTOR - 4	08/18/2007	1.10	<.52	0.33	<.064	<.049	<.042	0.53	0.80	4.87
COLLECTOR - 5	08/22/2007	0.44	<.52	0.20	<.064	<.049	<.042	0.11	0.31	1.83
COLLECTOR - 6	08/27/2007	0.23	<.52	<.11	<.064	<.049	<.042	<.093	0.16	0.48
COLLECTOR - 7	09/21/2007	1.00	<.52	0.36	<.064	<.049	<.042	0.34	0.76	4.83
COLLECTOR - 8	10/02/2007	0.64	<.52	0.23	<.064	<.049	<.042	0.23	0.48	2.83
COLLECTOR - 9	10/15/2007	0.13	<.52	<.093	<.064	<.049	<.042	<.093	<.11	0.19
COLLECTOR - 10	10/17/2007	0.18	<.52	0.12	<.064	<.049	<.042	<.093	0.14	0.52
COLLECTOR - 11	03/31/2008	9.60	<.52	2.90	<.064	0.12	0.06	4.20	7.10	42.92
COLLECTOR - 12	04/08/2008	1.00	<.52	0.40	<.064	<.049	<.042	0.42	0.69	4.61
COLLECTOR - 13	04/10/2008	2.10	<.52	0.65	<.064	<.049	<.042	0.95	1.60	9.53
COLLECTOR - 14	04/24/2008	8.40	<.52	2.80	<.064	0.07	<.042	4.50	5.90	37.19

Table 1–4. Concentrations of PAH compounds and total PAH summation for collector street—Continued.

[<, less than; —, data not available; all values expressed as micrograms per liter; chemical nomenclature is that of the Wisconsin State Laboratory of Hygiene]

Sample ID	Date	Acenaph- thene	Acenaph- thylene	Anthracene	Benzo (A) Anthracene	Benzo (A) Pyrene	Benzo (B) Fluoran- thene	Benzo (G,H,I.) Perylene	Benzo (K) Fluoran- thene	Chrysene	Dibenzo (A, H) Anthra- cene
COLLECTOR - 15	04/25/2008	<.064	<.11	<.063	0.35	0.49	0.69	0.58	0.27	0.59	<.078
COLLECTOR - 16	05/30/2008	<.064	<.11	<.031	0.24	0.40	0.53	0.47	0.20	0.41	<0.065
COLLECTOR - 17	06/05/2008	<.064	<.11	<.031	0.14	0.26	0.29	0.27	<.12	0.23	<0.038

Table 1–4. Concentrations of PAH compounds and total PAH summation for collector street—Continued.

[<, less than; —, data not available; all values expressed as micrograms per liter; chemical nomenclature is that of the Wisconsin State Laboratory of Hygiene]

Sample ID	Date	Fluoran- thene	Fluorene	Indeno (1,2,3-C,D) Pyrene	1-Methyl- naphthalene	2-Methyl- naphthalene	Naphthalene	Phenan- threne	Pyrene	Total PAH
COLLECTOR - 15	04/25/2008	1.50	<.52	0.59	<.064	<.049	<.042	0.68	1.10	6.84
COLLECTOR - 16	05/30/2008	1.00	<.52	0.48	<.064	<.049	<.042	0.36	0.75	4.84
COLLECTOR - 17	06/05/2008	0.54	<.52	0.29	<.064	<.049	<.042	0.18	0.41	2.61

Table 1–5. Concentrations of PAH compounds and total PAH summation for arterial street.

[<, less than; all values expressed as micrograms per liter; chemical nomenclature is that of the Wisconsin State Laboratory of Hygiene]

Sample ID	Date	Acenaphthene	Acenaphthylene	Anthracene	Benzo (A) Anthracene	Benzo (A) Pyrene	Benzo (B) Fluoranthene	Benzo (G,H,I,) Perylene	Benzo (K) Fluoranthene	Chrysene	Dibenzo (A, H) Anthracene
ARTERIAL - 1	05/11/2005	<.064	<.11	<.031	<.093	0.17	0.24	0.27	<.12	0.20	<.060
ARTERIAL - 2	05/19/2005	0.16	<.11	0.56	4.00	6.80	12.00	7.70	4.80	9.10	<1.2
ARTERIAL - 3	07/20/2005	<.064	<.11	0.31	1.90	3.70	5.10	4.20	2.40	4.30	<1.0
ARTERIAL - 4	07/21/2005	<.064	<.11	0.08	0.44	0.81	1.20	0.99	0.56	1.00	<.17
ARTERIAL - 5	04/29/2006	<.064	<.11	0.04	0.25	0.41	0.67	0.56	0.30	0.54	<.076
ARTERIAL - 6	05/09/2006	<.064	<.11	0.05	0.32	0.56	0.93	0.81	0.40	0.75	<.096
ARTERIAL - 7	05/11/2006	<.064	<.11	<.031	0.14	0.32	0.48	0.47	0.23	0.40	<.064
ARTERIAL - 8	05/24/2006	0.13	<.11	0.40	2.80	4.50	7.00	5.60	3.20	5.70	<.68
ARTERIAL - 9	06/09/2006	<.064	<.11	<.031	<.093	—	0.37	0.39	0.17	0.29	<.054
ARTERIAL - 10	06/25/2006	<.064	<.11	<.031	0.12	0.28	0.44	0.46	0.19	0.33	<.081
ARTERIAL - 11	07/11/2006	<.064	<.11	0.05	0.23	0.47	0.56	0.55	0.25	0.44	<.058

Table 1-5.   Concentrations of PAH compounds and total PAH summation for arterial street—Continued.

[<, less than; all values expressed as micrograms per liter; chemical nomenclature is that of the Wisconsin State Laboratory of Hygiene]

Sample ID	Date	Fluoran-thene	Fluorene	Indeno (1,2,3-C,D) Pyrene	1-Methyl-naphthalene	2-Methyl-naphthalene	Naphthalene	Phenan-threne	Pyrene	Total PAH
ARTERIAL - 1	05/11/2005	0.49	<.52	0.23	<.064	<.049	<.042	0.12	0.33	2.05
ARTERIAL - 2	05/19/2005	22.00	<.52	7.30	<.064	<.049	0.04	8.50	16.00	98.96
ARTERIAL - 3	07/29/2005	9.60	<.52	3.80	<.064	<.049	<.042	3.00	6.40	44.71
ARTERIAL - 4	07/21/2005	2.20	<.52	0.90	<.064	<.049	<.042	0.64	1.50	10.32
ARTERIAL - 5	04/29/2006	1.20	<.52	0.51	<.064	<.049	<.042	0.37	0.87	5.72
ARTERIAL - 6	05/09/2006	1.60	<.52	0.72	<.064	<.049	<.042	0.42	1.20	7.76
ARTERIAL - 7	05/11/2006	0.89	<.52	0.38	<.064	<.049	<.042	0.22	0.67	4.20
ARTERIAL - 8	05/24/2006	13.00	<.52	5.30	<.064	<.049	0.05	5.00	10.00	62.68
ARTERIAL - 9	06/09/2006	0.59	<.52	0.31	<.064	<.049	<.042	0.24	0.40	2.76
ARTERIAL - 10	06/25/2006	0.65	<.52	0.36	<.064	<.049	<.042	0.23	0.50	3.56
ARTERIAL - 11	07/11/2006	0.88	<.52	0.44	<.064	<.049	<.042	0.41	0.69	4.97

Table 1–6. Concentrations of PAH compounds and total PAH summation for commercial roof.

[<, less than; all values expressed as micrograms per liter; chemical nomenclature is that of the Wisconsin State Laboratory of Hygiene]

Sample ID	Date	Acenaph-thene	Acenaph-thylene	Anthracene	Benzo (A) Anthracene	Benzo (A) Pyrene	Benzo (B) Fluoran-thene	Benzo (G,H,I,) Perylene	Benzo (K) Fluoran-thene	Chrysene	Dibenzo (A, H) Anthra-cene
COMMERCIAL ROOF-1	08/17/2006	<.064	<.11	<.031	<.093	0.19	0.22	0.26	<.12	0.16	<.034
COMMERCIAL ROOF-2	08/28/2006	<.064	<.11	<.031	<.093	<.16	<.13	<.14	<.12	<0.031	<.034
COMMERCIAL ROOF-3	10/04/2006	<.064	<.11	<.031	<.093	0.24	0.27	0.24	<.12	0.21	<.034
COMMERCIAL ROOF-4	10/10/2006	<.064	<.11	<.031	0.16	0.29	0.33	0.29	<.12	0.27	<.034
COMMERCIAL ROOF-5	10/16/2006	<.064	<.11	<.031	0.11	0.21	0.23	0.20	<.12	0.17	<.034
COMMERCIAL ROOF-6	10/21/2006	<.064	<.11	<.031	<.093	0.18	0.20	0.17	<.12	0.15	<.034
COMMERCIAL ROOF-7	03/21/2007	<.064	<.11	0.09	0.58	0.99	1.30	1.10	0.62	1.10	<0.12
COMMERCIAL ROOF-8	04/02/2007	<.064	<.11	<.031	0.12	0.20	0.24	0.22	<.12	0.19	<.034
COMMERCIAL ROOF-9	04/22/2007	<.064	<.11	<.031	0.10	0.23	0.32	0.31	0.17	0.30	<.034

Table 1–6.   Concentrations of PAH compounds and total PAH summation for commercial roof—Continued.

[<, less than; all values expressed as micrograms per liter; chemical nomenclature is that of the Wisconsin State Laboratory of Hygiene]

Sample ID	Date	Fluoran- thene	Fluorene	Indeno (1,2,3-C,D) Pyrene	1-Methyl- naphthalene	2-Methyl- naphthalene	Naphthalene	Phenan- threne	Pyrene	Total PAH
COMMERCIAL ROOF-1	08/17/2006	0.38	<.52	0.21	<.064	<.049	<.042	0.15	0.31	1.88
COMMERCIAL ROOF-2	08/28/2006	0.12	<.52	<.093	<.064	<.049	<.042	<.093	<.11	0.12
COMMERCIAL ROOF-3	10/04/2006	0.54	<.52	0.24	<.064	<.049	<.042	0.23	0.43	2.40
COMMERCIAL ROOF-4	10/10/2006	0.72	<.52	0.27	<.064	<.049	<.042	0.32	0.56	3.21
COMMERCIAL ROOF-5	10/16/2006	0.46	<.52	0.17	<.064	<.049	<.042	0.23	0.37	2.15
COMMERCIAL ROOF-6	10/21/2006	0.46	<.52	<0.14	<.064	<.049	<.042	0.31	0.36	1.83
COMMERCIAL ROOF-7	03/21/2007	2.90	<.52	1.00	<.064	<.049	<.042	1.60	2.30	13.58
COMMERCIAL ROOF-8	04/02/2007	0.53	<.52	0.20	<.064	<.049	<.042	0.28	0.42	2.40
COMMERCIAL ROOF-9	04/22/2007	0.73	<.52	0.31	<.064	<.049	<.042	0.33	0.56	3.36

Table 1–7.   Concentrations of PAH compounds and total PAH summation for a mixed-use area (strip mall).

[<, less than; all values expressed as micrograms per liter; chemical nomenclature is that of the Wisconsin State Laboratory of Hygiene]

Sample ID	Date	Acenaph-thene	Acenaph-thylene	Anthracene	Benzo (A) Anthracene	Benzo (A) Pyrene	Benzo (B) Fluoran-thene	Benzo (G,H,I,) Perylene	Benzo (K) Fluoran-thene	Chrysene	Dibenzo (A, H) Anthra-cene
MIXED USE - 1	04/08/2008	<.064	<.11	<.031	0.22	0.49	1.10	1.00	0.49	0.82	<.15
MIXED USE - 2	04/10/2008	<.064	<.11	<.094	0.47	0.85	1.60	1.40	0.53	1.20	<.17
MIXED USE - 3	05/29/2008	<.064	<.11	<.031	0.09	0.18	0.25	0.25	<.12	0.17	<.034
MIXED USE - 4	06/05/2008	<.064	<.11	<.031	0.22	0.44	0.75	0.76	0.25	0.52	<.090
MIXED USE - 5	06/12/2008	<.064	<.11	<.031	0.09	0.16	0.21	0.23	<.12	0.15	<.034
MIXED USE - 6	06/12/2008	<.064	<.11	<.031	0.09	<.16	0.13	<.14	<.12	0.08	<.034
MIXED USE - 7	06/22/2008	<.064	<.11	<.031	0.11	0.18	0.57	0.62	0.16	0.45	<.066
MIXED USE - 8	07/07/2008	<.064	<.11	<.031	0.09	<.16	0.21	0.23	<.12	0.15	<.034
MIXED USE - 9	07/10/2008	<.064	<.11	<.031	0.09	<.16	0.21	0.23	<.12	0.15	<.034
MIXED USE - 10	07/11/2008	<.064	<.11	<.031	0.15	0.32	0.55	0.56	0.17	0.38	<.065
MIXED USE - 11	07/19/2008	<.064	<.11	<.031	0.09	<.16	<.13	<.14	<.12	0.04	<.034
MIXED USE - 12	08/04/2008	<.064	<.11	<.060	0.39	0.47	0.60	0.51	0.23	0.61	<.065
MIXED USE - 13	08/13/2008	<.064	<.11	<.031	0.41	0.71	0.99	0.90	0.35	0.88	<.11
MIXED USE - 14	08/08/2028	<.064	<.11	<.031	0.39	1.00	1.40	1.30	0.45	1.10	<.13
MIXED USE - 15	09/04/2008	<.064	<.11	<.031	0.45	0.91	1.60	1.40	0.51	1.40	<.16

Table 1–7. Concentrations of PAH compounds and total PAH summation for a mixed-use area (strip mall)—Continued.

[<, less than; all values expressed as micrograms per liter; chemical nomenclature is that of the Wisconsin State Laboratory of Hygiene]

Sample ID	Date	Fluoran-thene	Fluorene	Indeno (1,2,3-C,D) Pyrene	1-Methyl-naphthalene	2-Methyl-naphthalene	Naphthalene	Phenan-threne	Pyrene	Total PAH
MIXED USE - 1	04/08/2008	1.90	<.52	0.83	<.064	<.049	<.042	0.47	1.30	8.62
MIXED USE - 2	04/10/2008	2.80	<.52	1.40	<.064	<.049	<.042	0.97	1.90	13.12
MIXED USE - 3	05/29/2008	0.35	<.52	0.23	<.064	<.049	<.042	<.093	0.24	1.76
MIXED USE - 4	06/05/2008	1.10	<.52	0.70	<.064	<.049	<.042	0.36	0.82	5.92
MIXED USE - 5	06/12/2008	0.31	<.52	0.21	<.064	<.049	<.042	<.093	0.22	1.58
MIXED USE - 6	06/12/2008	0.18	<.52	0.13	<.064	<.049	<.042	<.093	0.13	0.74
MIXED USE - 7	06/22/2008	0.79	<.52	0.57	<.064	<.049	<.042	0.26	0.50	4.21
MIXED USE - 8	07/07/2008	0.28	<.52	0.22	<.064	<.049	<.042	<.093	0.21	1.39
MIXED USE - 9	07/10/2008	0.28	<.52	0.22	<.064	<.049	<.042	<.093	0.21	1.39
MIXED USE - 10	07/11/2008	0.72	<.52	0.55	<.064	<.049	<.042	0.25	0.53	4.18
MIXED USE - 11	07/19/2008	<.11	<.52	<.095	<.064	<.049	<.042	<.093	<.11	0.14
MIXED USE - 12	08/04/2008	2.20	<.52	0.51	<.064	<.049	<.042	0.52	1.50	7.54
MIXED USE - 13	08/13/2008	2.50	<.52	0.88	<.064	<.049	<.042	0.82	1.70	10.14
MIXED USE - 14	08/08/2028	2.50	<.52	1.20	<.064	<.049	<.042	0.52	1.80	11.66
MIXED USE - 15	09/04/2008	3.70	<.52	1.40	<.064	<.049	<.042	1.20	2.20	14.77

Table 1–7.   Concentrations of PAH compounds and total PAH summation for a mixed-use area (strip mall)—Continued.

[<, less than; all values expressed as micrograms per liter; chemical nomenclature is that of the Wisconsin State Laboratory of Hygiene]

Sample ID	Date	Acenaphthene	Acenaphthylene	Anthracene	Benzo (A) Anthracene	Benzo (A) Pyrene	Benzo (B) Fluoranthene	Benzo (G,H,I,) Perylene	Benzo (K) Fluoranthene	Chrysene	Dibenzo (A, H) Anthracene
MIXED USE - 16	09/08/2008	<.064	<.11	<.031	0.12	0.30	0.54	0.46	0.18	0.47	<.056
MIXED USE - 17	09/12/2008	<.064	<.11	<.031	0.13	0.28	0.63	0.49	0.20	0.62	<.059
MIXED USE - 18	10/07/2008	<.064	<.11	<.031	0.38	1.20	1.70	1.70	0.52	1.30	<.16
MIXED USE - 19	10/15/2008	<.064	<.11	<.031	0.15	0.56	0.80	0.78	0.25	0.65	<.078

Table 1–7.   Concentrations of PAH compounds and total PAH summation for a mixed-use area (strip mall)—Continued.

[<, less than; all values expressed as micrograms per liter; chemical nomenclature is that of the Wisconsin State Laboratory of Hygiene]

Sample ID	Date	Fluoranthene	Fluorene	Indeno (1,2,3-C,D) Pyrene	1-Methyl-naphthalene	2-Methyl-naphthalene	Naphthalene	Phenanthrene	Pyrene	Total PAH
MIXED USE - 16	09/08/2008	1.20	<.52	0.47	<.064	<.049	<.042	0.31	<.70	4.05
MIXED USE - 17	09/12/2008	1.50	<.52	0.55	<.064	<.049	<.042	0.48	0.84	5.72
MIXED USE - 18	10/07/2008	3.10	<.52	1.50	<.064	<.049	<.042	0.82	2.00	14.22
MIXED USE - 19	10/15/2008	1.50	<.52	0.71	<.064	<.049	<.042	0.47	0.91	6.78